DACH
AND
DACHSHUNDS

Dachshund
Total Guide

Dachshund: From Dachshund Puppies to Dachshund Dogs,
Dachshund Health, Dachshund Training, Dachshund
Socialization, Dachshund Breeders & Rescue, Showing & More!

Susanne Saben

© DYM Worldwide Publishers

Published by DYM Worldwide Publishers.

ISBN: 978-1-911355-79-3

3

DYM Worldwide Publishers takes no responsibility for, and will not be liable for, the websites being temporarily or being removed from the Internet. The accuracy and completeness of the information provided herein, and opinions stated herein are not guaranteed or warranted to produce any particular results, and the advice or strategies, contained herein may not be suitable for every individual. The author, publisher, distributors, and/or affiliates shall not be liable for any loss incurred as a consequence of the use and application, directly or indirectly of any information presented in this work. This publication is designed to provide information regarding the subject matter covered. The information included in this book has been compiled to give an overview of the topics covered. The information contained in this book has been compiled to provide an overview of the subject. It is not intended as medical advice and should not be construed as such. For a firm diagnosis of any medical conditions, you should consult a doctor or veterinarian (as related to animal health). The writer, publisher, distributors, and/or affiliates of this work are not responsible for any damages or negative consequences following any of the treatments or methods highlighted in this book.

Website links are for informational purposes only and should not be seen as a personal endorsement; the same applies to any products or services mentioned in this work. The reader should also be aware that although the web links included were correct at the time of writing they may become out of date in the future. Any pricing or currency exchange rate information was accurate at the time of writing but may become out of date in the future. The Author, Publisher, distributors, and/or affiliates assume no responsibility for pricing and currency exchange rates mentioned within this work.

Table of Contents

Introduction 10
Chapter 1 – Meet the Dachshund..12
What is the History of the Dachshund Dog?..........12
What was the Dachshund Bred for?......................13
Do Dachshunds Make Good Hunting Dogs? 14
Chapter 2 – Is the Dachshund Right for You?......................15
Is the Dachshund a Good Companion?..................16
What is the General Temperament of the
Dachshund? 17
Will the Dachshund Require Much Maintenance? ..18
What is the Appropriate Amount of Exercise for
the Dachshund? 20
What Is Typical Dachshund Behavior? 21
Do Dachshunds Get Along with Other Animals? ..23
What is the Average Weight of the Dachshund? 24
Approximately How Large is a Full-Grown
Dachshund? 24
What is the Typical Cost of a Dachshund?.............25
What is Involved in Being a Dachshund Owner?....25
Should I Invest in a Puppy or an Adult Dachshund?...26
Is a Senior Dachshund a Good Investment? 28
Chapter 3 – What are the Accepted Breed Standards for the
Dachshund? 29
What is the height and weight of a Standard-sized
Dachshund? 29

Is there a Miniature Dachshund? 32

Miniature versus Toy versus Teacup Dachshunds ..32

Wire-haired Dachshund Standards......................33

Long-haired Dachshunds and Accepted Colors 34

Typical Colors of a Dachshund: 35

    Red Dachshund 35

    Black 36

    Brown 36

    Piebald 36

    Tan 37

    Black and Tan.. 37

    Brindle 38

    Blue... 38

    Dapple 38

    White... 39

    Merle 39

    Chocolate... 39

    Sable 40

    Gray 40

    Blue and Tan 40

    Spotted Dachshund 41

Other Dachshund Colors: Dapple Piebald, Isabella and Tan, Fawn, Brown Dapple, English Cream 41

Chapter 4 – Where Can I Buy a Dachshund? 43

Dachshund Puppies for Sale – Finding Breeders....43

How Can I Find Reputable Dachshund Breeders? ...44

Where Can I Find Dachshunds and Dachshund Puppies (Weiner Dogs) for Sale Near Me? 47

How do I Find Long Haired Dachshund Puppies for Sale Near Me? 48

Is it Possible to Find a Miniature Dachshund
for Sale? 48

What is the Average Miniature Dachshund Price? ...48

How Do I Find Reputable Miniature Dachshund
Breeders? 49

How About Standard Dachshunds and Standard
Dachshund Puppies for Sale? 49

Where Can I Find Wire-haired Dachshund
Breeders? 50

Where Can I Find Cream Dachshund Puppies or
Piebald Patterned Puppies for Sale? 50

How Difficult is it to Find Dapple Dachshund
Puppies for Sale? 50

Chapter 5 – Should I Consider Adopting a Dachshund? 51

How Do I Find a Dachshund Rescue or
Dachshunds for Adoption Near Me? 51

How Difficult is it to Find Dachshund Puppies
for Adoption? 52

Where Can I Find a Miniature Dachshund Rescue
or Mini Dachshunds for Adoption? 52

Are there Rescues Devoted Specifically to Dapple
Dachshund Rescue Dogs? 53

Is there such a Thing as a Dachshund Sanctuary?
Is it Possible to Adopt from One? 53

Chapter 6 – What Items Will I Need in Order to Care for my
Dachshund? 55

What Type of Dog Food is Best for my
Dachshund? 55

Should I Make my own Dachshund Dog Food? 59

How Can I Be Sure I Have Purchased Healthy
Dog Treats for my Dachshund? 61

What Should I Look for When Purchasing a Dog Bed for my Dachshund?..62

What is the Best Type of Dachshund Puppy Food?...63

Harness vs. Dachshund Dog Collar 66

Measuring Your Doxie: 66

What are Top Recommendations for a Dachshund Dog Leash? 67

What are the Best Dachshund Dog Toys?..............68

Will I Need to Purchase a Dachshund House? 69

Dachshund Carriers and Dog Crates 69

Dachshund Pet Gates – Are they Necessary?..........72

Will my Dachshund Need Supplements or Vitamins?...72

What Items will I Need to Keep My Dachshund Clean: Shampoo, Brush, other Care Items 73

What Other Items will I Need to Purchase Before Bringing my Dachshund Home (Dachshund Dog Bowls, Kennels, Products and Accessories)?..........76

Dachshund Dog Crate 76

Chapter 7 – What Should I Consider When Purchasing a Dachshund? 79

What Vaccinations can I Expect my Dachshund Puppy to Receive?..79

Is the Dachshund Good with Kids?.......................82

Does the Dachshund Experience any Health Issues?...83

What Makes the Dachshund Muzzle Special?........85

Chapter 8 – What is Involved in Breeding and Raising Dachshunds?...86

Chapter 9 – What is Involved in Showing Dachshunds?............90

Chapter 10 – Senior Dachshunds 93

Chapter 11 – What Will Training a Dachshund Include?............97

Dachshund Puppy Training 97

Dachshund Dog Harness and Leash Training......100

Dachshund Crate/Kennel Training 101

Chapter 12 – What are Some Examples of Dachshund Mixes? ..103

Dachshund Beagle Mix 103

Dachshund Terrier Mix...104

Corgi Dachshund Mix..105

French Bulldog Dachshund 106

English Dachshund..106

Other Dachshund Mixes 107

Conclusion 111

BONUS CHAPTER 112

Dachshund Breeders in the USA 112

Dachshund Breeders in Canada...........................115

Dachshund Breeders and UK Resources 117

Introduction

Welcome to the wonderful world of Dachshunds! The Dachshund is often referred to as a "weenie dog" because of its long, narrow body. H.L. Mencken described the Dachshund as "a half-dog high and a dog-and-a-half long." Of course, there is more than meets the eye when it comes to this tiny pooch! The Dachshund was originally developed in Germany, where he was used as a scent hound. In fact, his name literally translates to "badger dog." He has generally been used as a companion dog, but, he was bred to scent and flush out prey. He is also used, on occasion, to track wounded animals.

Doxies come in a variety of coats and colors. The three main types of Dachshunds are the short-haired, the long-haired, and wire-haired variations. Colors range from a deep, dark red solid to a variety of unique patterns. This is part of the appeal of the breed. There is something about the Dachshund that is appealing to all types of dog lovers.

The Dachshund's personality is just as unique as his one of a kind as his appearance. The American Kennel Club describes the Doxie as "spunky," which is quite true! The Doxie is also known to be a tad stubborn at times, but patience and persistence will reward your efforts when training the Dachshund. Of course, I plan to share plenty of helpful tips, as well, within this book!

You made the right decision when it comes to purchasing a pup that is fun, smart, and a great all-around companion! Here's to many enjoyable years with your new canine buddy!

Figure 1 - The Dachshund has a long, slender body, which makes him perfect for burrowing into holes in search of prey.

CHAPTER 1

Meet the Dachshund

What is the History of the Dachshund Dog?

The Dachshund is native to Germany, where it was bred to assist in flushing out small prey. Artwork depicting the Doxie dates back to the fifteenth century, and historical documents mention an "earth dog" or the "badger creeper." Modern Germany refers to the Dachshund as the "Teckel" or the "Dachsel."

The early Dachshund came in a variety of sizes. A larger Doxie, weighing approximately thirty-five pounds, was used when hunting badgers. Packs of this size of Dachshund were also utilized when tracking and taking down a wild boar. A Doxie approximately fifteen to twenty pounds aided in flushing out den animals, such as the fox. This size of Dachshund was also appropriate for deer hunting. The much smaller version, often referred to as the *kaninchen* (a German word meaning "rabbit"), accompanies rabbit hunters. This size Doxie has also been known to hunt weasels. Although the Dachshund was always bred for hunting, over time, he was developed into the smaller dog that most are familiar with today. We will delve into the size variations of the Doxie in forthcoming chapters.

As the utilization of the Dachshund changed, so did the breed's development and purpose. By the 1800s, the Doxie was becoming more of a companion animal than a hunting hound. In fact, dog aficionado and breeder Queen Victoria had a hand in this transition of the Dachshund. By the latter part of the century, the Doxie had been reduced from a thirty-five-pound pup (on average) to twenty to twenty-five pounds. The first Doxie was registered with the American Kennel Club in 1885, and the breed's popularity soared in the United States (he was already quite popular in Europe, particularly in royal households). By the 1950s, the Dachshund was one of the top family companion dogs in the United States, and the Doxie still holds this distinction. Only in parts of Europe is the Dachshund utilized for hunting purposes. However, the Doxie's popularity holds strong throughout America and Europe due to his dynamic personality, and one-of-a-kind looks.

What was the Dachshund Bred for?

The Dachshund's name literally means "badger dog," and he was a fearless, tenacious little hunter. His long nose aided him in picking up the scent of his prey; his long body gave him the ability to slide into the burrows and dens of said prey. His sturdy little legs are powerful diggers, and the bold little pup often dug out and dove into holes after foxes, rabbits, and badgers. His human hunting companions often used his long, straight tail as a "handle" of sorts – if the dog went a little too far into the hole, the hunter could pull him out with the tail.

Do Dachshunds Make Good Hunting Dogs?

The American Kennel Club describes the Dachshund as the only hound in their registry that hunts both above and below ground. This distinction is owed to the fact that Dachshunds were utilized to hunt many different types of prey.

In fact, the elongated body of the Doxie is what made the breed so sought after when hunters chose a hunting companion. The short legs of the Dachshund are powerful digging machines; he employs them to reach deep into the burrows and dens of foxes and badgers. His elongated snout makes him one of the best of the scent hounds. Yes, the Dachshund was a supreme hunting dog, even if he was one of the smallest of all the hounds.

CHAPTER 2

Is the Dachshund Right for You?

What makes the Dachshund special? Why should you choose the Dachshund over other breeds? First, the Dachshund is not only unique because of his elongated body, but, many times, no two Doxies are exactly alike! There are fifteen, yes, *fifteen*, variations of coat colors. If you want a dog that is not quite like others, the Dachshund will provide this to you simply because of his appearance! In addition, the Dachshund is a superb watchdog. He will alert his owners to anything amiss in his territory (i.e., your property). He is extremely intelligent, and, once he is housebroken, the Doxie makes an entertaining companion dog. Speaking of companionship, the Dachshund tends to live between fourteen and sixteen years of age; that is, on average, at least two years longer than other small breed dogs. The Doxie can be quite the clown, and, for this reason, many Dachshund owners say that once a person owns a Doxie, they will want more! Let's look a little more in-depth at Dachshund traits that make them such wonderful dogs.

Figure 2 The Doxie thrives on a relationship with his owner.

Is the Dachshund a Good Companion?

The Doxie makes a great family dog, and he loves children. He is also perfect for singles or empty-nesters. In fact, sometimes the Dachshund does better with one owner. This is not to say that he will not do well with a couple or a family. On the contrary, the Doxie has a tendency to bond to one person, but, he can also be very loyal to a family with children of any age. He is protective of all members of his family.

The Dachshund is happy in a home with a large yard or an apartment with limited outdoor space. This adds to the fact that the Doxie is a good match for many people. He will enjoy – and thrives on – playtime with you; however, he is just as happy spending time sitting in your lap on the couch. This means that the Doxie fits a wide variety of human lifestyles and energy levels. Furthermore, the intelligence of the Dachshund cannot be matched. Years of development as a hunting dog only added to the smarts of the Doxie. He watches his owner for commands, even though at times he may seem to go his own way, so to speak. Some owners compare the Dachshund and his interaction with his owners, as one similar to a cat. The Doxie thrives on cuddles, belly rubs, back scratches, and overall general affection from their humans. At times, he can be somewhat independent, but this trait is often admired in the Dachshund. In addition, his propensity for loyalty makes him the perfect fit for most any person's lifestyle.

What is the General Temperament of the Dachshund?

The Dachshund has quite a dynamic personality! Most owners describe him as a bit of a clown, in addition to being a wonderful cuddle-buddy. He is highly energetic as well as extremely intelligent. This means that he can become bored easily; however, he can be occupied with toys that stimulate his mind and body.

The Doxie is considered to be a good choice for families with children. However, he does better with children who understand that he must be carried properly or risk damage to his elongated spine. Otherwise, his energy will match any child's, and he makes a fun companion for young ones. The Dachshund also gets along with other dogs; however, experts recommend early socialization so that your pup will know how to behave around other dogs. The Doxie is somewhat territorial; he will alert you to anything or anyone he believes is invading his sacred space.

It should be remembered that the Doxie is a hunter at heart. He was bred to chase certain prey (you may find that the Dachshund chases cats and squirrels while outside), and he has a need to dig that was developed by his ancestors. Certainly, the Dachshund should never be left alone outside to spend the primary part of his day; however, you may want to allow him time in a fenced-in area for exercise. Keep in mind that he does enjoy digging when building your fence. By placing your boards a little deeper in the ground, you will discourage him from digging out and escaping the security of your yard.

Figure 3 The Dachshund is energetic, and he loves to play with other pups.

Will the Dachshund Require Much Maintenance?

The Doxie sheds only seasonally, and a smooth-coated Dachshund requires very little in the way of grooming. Brushing him with a bristle brush at least once a week will remove any dirt from his fur. It will also stimulate natural oils in the coat, leaving your Doxie shiny and healthy looking!

Most groomers agree that the best type of brush for a short-haired pup is the bristle brush. In fact, experts recommend a brush made with boar bristles. This is a more natural type of brush, compared to one made with synthetic bristles. It is also softer, gentler, and will not irritate the skin of your Dachshund. Other than a weekly brushing, your pup will not need much more in the way of grooming. The longer-haired Doxie, however, requires more attention than his short-haired companion.

First, the long-haired Dachshund will require daily brushing. The long-haired Doxie has a double coat. His outer coat is fine, but the undercoat is short and fluffy and will need attention in order to prevent matting. It is recommended that you utilize a pin brush for this type of pup (be sure that the bristles of the pin brush have round cushions so as not to irritate the skin of your dog). Experts recommend that you be especially vigilant in brushing the long hair around the legs, sides, and stomach of the long-haired Doxie, as this area is close to the ground and more apt to pick up debris. One should always start brushing a long-haired Doxie at the nape of the neck and work down to the sides and stomach.

A long-haired Dachshund will also require monthly bathing (unless, of course, he finds something muddy or stinky to roll in between his monthly washing). It is always best to choose an all-natural shampoo, particularly an aloe or oatmeal type.

You may or may not choose to have your long-haired Doxie trimmed by a professional. However, you can do this trimming on your own, as the Dachshund has a natural pattern of growth that lends to an easy trim. He will also need his nails trimmed every two weeks.

What is the Appropriate Amount of Exercise for the Dachshund?

The Dachshund is a high-energy little dog, and, in order to keep him from getting into mischief, owners should provide an appropriate amount of exercise.

When the Doxie is a puppy, he will need short intervals of exercise. Starting when he is about four months old, take him out on the leash for about five minutes at a time. This will help him learn how to not only walk on the leash but also to become accustomed to traffic as well. Two or three short walks a day will suffice.

Once the Doxie becomes acclimated to his leash, and to what is expected of him when outdoors, then you may increase his walking time. By the time he is six months of age, try to have him accustomed to a fifteen-to-twenty-minute walk, once or twice a day. Continue increasing his walking time by just a few minutes every two or three weeks. As he approaches one year of age, the Dachshund should be used to walking around forty-five minutes, to one hour daily. It is best to split this walking time into two or three shorter sessions throughout the day.

Owners must also consider the idea that the Doxie needs mental exercise as much as he needs physical activity. There are a wealth of toys that satisfy the Dachshund's need to chew and provide other mental stimulation. Regardless of how you provide mental activity for your Doxie, be assured that he needs the mental stimulation as much as he needs the physical exercise.

What is Typical Dachshund Behavior?

The Dachshund is generally a pleasant, happy dog. He can be somewhat stubborn at times; however, dedicated Doxie owners find that patience and persistence pay off when molding the Dachshund to become the dog you want him to be. The Doxie is naturally curious. One can never forget that he is a hound at heart and a scent hound at that. This means that he will follow a trail should he be left unattended outside.

In many ways, the Doxie is much like a terrier even though he is technically a hound. He expects to be a part of everything you do. He is also somewhat territorial, and he will chase squirrels, cats, and other small animals if you allow him to roam outside without a leash. He is reputed to be somewhat jealous of his toys as well. Experts recommend putting a stop to this behavior as soon as you observe it. One way to do this is to "trade" something with your pup for the toy. Always present something more rewarding than the toy; for instance, a treat or a piece of meat. The object is to teach your pup that when he gives up the toy, something better is in store. Over time, this will help the dog become more approachable when he is playing with toys, or even eating. It also teaches the dog a bit of self-control and may aid him in being a better-behaved dog.

Doxies are notorious when it comes to barking. He will alert you to anything amiss in what he perceives to be his territory, and, if he is left alone a good bit, his tendency to bark increases. (Some owners often purchase Dachshunds in pairs for this reason, in order to prevent loneliness and boredom.)

Dachshunds love to be the center of attention! The Doxie will watch your behavior, and, if he believes that he is entertaining you, he will continue whatever clownish activity is making you laugh.

Conversely, he is just as happy to cuddle with you on the couch. However, do not allow the Doxie to become lazy – which he might be inclined to do. The Dachshund is prone to gaining weight should he not receive ample exercise. Often, the Dachshund will enjoy simply experiencing playtime with you. Games of fetch will not only give your pup physical activity but time spent together will also increase the bond between you and your Doxie.

Overall, the Dachshund is a loyal dog who loves his family, and he enjoys being a part of family activities. He is a fun-loving pup that will do almost anything to win (and keep) your attention. He loves to play games, but, most of all, he loves interacting with people. The Doxie is the type of dog that owners "get addicted" to – once they own one, they do not care to have any other breed of pup! The joy that a Dachshund brings his owners is beyond compare!

Do Dachshunds Get Along with Other Animals?

Dachshunds may be hounds, but they often behave more like a terrier, in that they are territorial. Not only does this behavior extend to toys and food (and sometimes to their owners), it tends to make the Doxie somewhat less friendly with other animals. Have no fear, though, this behavior can be corrected with early socialization.

Early socialization is the most basic form of dog training. It involves allowing your pup to be around responsible children and a variety of animals so that the Doxie learns what type of behavior you expect from him. Socialization should begin from the moment that you bring your Doxie pup home. If no children are in your home, invite the children of friends, or family members, over on occasion to play with the new dog. Again, any children you allow to play with your Dachshund should know that he can suffer an injury to his back if he is not held properly (we will discuss this further in a subsequent chapter). Games of fetch or tug of war might be appropriate for a growing puppy. In addition, a puppy should be allowed to interact with other dogs and cats as soon as possible (I recommend waiting until the pup is at least three months old. Any younger and the puppy is really too small to play appropriately.) Early socialization with different people and animals is nothing but beneficial to your new Doxie, and giving him these opportunities will demonstrate how you want him to act as he matures into adulthood.

Figure 4 Doxies get along well with other animals if socialized early.

What is the Average Weight of the Dachshund?

The average Dachshund weighs approximately twenty to thirty pounds (9kg to 13.6kg). A miniature Doxie weighs about eleven pounds (4.98kg).

Approximately How Large is a Full-Grown Dachshund?

A mature Dachshund may weigh up to thirty pounds (and he may be as little as fifteen pounds). He is also generally eight to eleven inches (20 - 27cm) in height. Minis may be five to seven (13 - 18 cm) inches tall.

What is the Typical Cost of a Dachshund?

A registered Dachshund (one with papers) generally costs anywhere from $300.00 to $750.00. Some breeders may charge less for a male pup; a registered male may cost between $250.00 and $500.00. A Doxie without papers may cost anywhere from $50.00 to $200.00. To be sure, factors such as gender, location, and the quality of the dog will have some influence on the price.

What is Involved in Being a Dachshund Owner?

Some experts claim that people don't train their Doxies; the Dachshund trains its owner on how to live with him! Certainly, those who own Doxies often say they could never see themselves owning any other breed, and this is due to the dog's innate ability to both entertain you and love you back in his own special way. There are certain things one should remember when dealing with a Dachshund. The Doxie is born and bred to be a hunter. This means that he is tenacious and thinks independently. Never underestimate just how intelligent the Doxie is! He may figure out some things that you don't necessarily want him to, such as how to get to food or how to get out of an enclosure. Training the Dachshund is often challenging, but it can be done. The Doxie might take a little longer than some other breeds to complete housebreaking due to his independent nature.

Owners must also be cautious that the Dachshund does not jump down from high objects; some owners will attach doggie steps to the bed and to the front porch so that jumping is kept to a minimum. In addition, to help prevent your Doxie from injuring his spine, always try to support his elongated back.

Dachshunds also have a tendency to eat things that they shouldn't. Caution children not to leave pencils or toys lying around, and never leave food unattended as certain foods can be toxic to your pup. If a Doxie chews and swallows certain objects – such as parts of a pen or pencil or pieces of rubber toys – it may have to have surgery to correct a bowel obstruction. Remember, an ounce of prevention is worth a pound of cure!

Because Dachshunds are prone to weight gain, you should always monitor their diet. Never let the wily Doxie fool you – he will always act as if he is hungry, but it is up to you as the pet parent to feed him the appropriate amount of food, based on his size. At the same time, one should ensure that the Dachshund gets plenty of exercise. An adult Doxie needs up to one hour per day. This need not be long walks outside! One can use toys indoors to facilitate physical activity as well.

Finally, a Dachshund must *always* be on a leash while outdoors (unless, of course, he is in a proper enclosure). The Doxie has a high prey drive, and he will chase anything he deems as prey. A little bit of caution will prevent this however!

Should I Invest in a Puppy or an Adult Dachshund?

This is a very personal decision. Only you can determine exactly what age Doxie is right for you, but with a little information you can make the right choice for you.

The advantages of adopting an older Dachshund may include the fact that the dog is already housebroken (this is NOT a guarantee of completed potty training; however, some experts say that owners will work with their Doxies throughout their lifetimes on housebreaking). Also, if an older Dachshund has any health problems, you will know from the beginning exactly what to expect.

Dachshunds are very loyal to all members of their family, but often, the Doxie will bond to one person in particular. Adult Dachshunds may have slightly more trouble acclimating to your family due to this fact. This might be something to consider when preparing to bring an adult Dachshund into your home.

One should remember that when you acquire a puppy, you are not fully sure exactly what type of dog he will turn out to be. Although a reputable breeder will ensure through testing that their pups do not have any genetically-transmitted diseases, the breeder cannot always guarantee a clean bill of health for your new puppy. In addition, when bringing home a puppy, you cannot be sure of the exact size and temperament of the dog as it approaches adulthood.

At the same time, when you choose to purchase a puppy, you will play a pivotal role in shaping the behavior of your dog. If you are reticent about training your pup yourself, you can always send him to obedience classes.

Another option is adopting (or purchasing) what is considered an "adolescent" dog. This age ranges from eight months to twenty-four months.

Should you wish to have a dog whose behavior and training is already established, then purchasing an adult dog might be the right option for you. If you think you would rather work with your puppy to make him what you wish him to be, then choosing a puppy (preferably one that is eight weeks or older) is the way to go. He will be old enough to be away from his mother, and he is also more apt to take to housebreaking and other training, than a six-week-old pup.

Is a Senior Dachshund a Good Investment?

Doxies live up to sixteen years on average. This makes the Dachshund one of the longest living dog breeds. Yes, if you can obtain a senior Doxie (eight years old or older), then, provided the dog is able to maintain good health, you may have your Dachshund for a number of years – sometimes as long as other dog owners of a different breed! (The Great Dane is considered a senior dog at age five, by comparison.)

CHAPTER 3

What are the Accepted Breed Standards for the Dachshund?

What is the Height and Weight of a Standard-sized Dachshund?

A Standard-sized Doxie generally weighs between sixteen and thirty-two pounds. His height is generally eight to eleven inches (20 – 27 cm).

Should you consider showing your Dachshund, it is a good idea to know what the breed standards are regarding the appearance of your pup. The Dachshund Club of America has developed a set of standards by which the breed is judged in the show ring.

First, the Doxie is considered "low to the ground," with a long body and characteristically short, yet powerful little legs. One interesting standard states that his skin will be somewhat elastic, and he will not have excessive wrinkles. He should appear intelligent and alert to the judges (imagine him ready to dig a fox out of its burrow).

His head should appear to taper from the base of the skull to the tip of the nose when viewed from the side or above (as a judge would view him). His eyes are almond-shaped, and not too large. He should also not appear to be "beady-eyed." His ears will be set near the top of his head, and they should be of moderate length; they should be rounded at the tip, not pointed, nor should they be narrow or folded. His nose will almost be "Roman" in appearance (a slight arch in the muzzle). His teeth should be strong and powerful in appearance, and they will ideally meet in a scissors-type bite. His neck should be long, muscular, and free of dewlap.

His back, when viewed in profile, should be in as straight a line as possible. His chest is deep and muscular in order for him to properly dig out prey. His shoulder blades are long and broad and should be set at the thorax. His upper arm and his forearm will appear strong and muscular; although they are rather short, this area will appear mighty powerful. His hindquarters will also appear to be quite muscular. His pelvis, thigh, and rear pastern will all come together to appear as a right angle. He should have five toes, and the dewclaws may or may not be removed. The pads of his feet should be thick and tough. His rear feet will be somewhat smaller than his front paws but will also be thick and tough.

Attention should also be paid to the three varieties of the Dachshund: the smooth coat, the wirehaired coat, and the longhaired coat.

The smooth Dachshund should possess a smooth, shiny coat which is close to the body. The hair of a smooth coat is short and fine. A smooth-coat Doxie should not have a bushy tail or one that is partially or entirely hairless.

The wirehaired Dachshund will have a top coat that is short, thick, and almost hard. He will also possess an undercoat which is short and fine. He will also sport what appears to be a "beard" and bushy eyebrows. His jaw and ears will not have the bushy hair of the rest of the body. His hair should not stick out irregularly, and there should never be long, curly, or wavy hair in his coat. He should not have a "flag" tail (the tail should not stand at an erect position with long hair on the tail).

The longhaired Doxie possesses sleek, shiny hair which often appears wavy. His hair will be especially long on the neck, chest, and on the underside of the body as well as the legs. The hair on his ears should also be long. The Dachshund can be a variety of colors, which will be discussed further in this chapter.

Figure 5: Common Dachshund coloring. Notice the rounded ears, the muscular chest, and the tapered tail.

Is there a Miniature Dachshund?

Yes, and the Mini Doxie is held to basically the same show standards as the standard Dachshund. However, the Miniature Dachshund competes in a different division from the standard Doxie. The Mini Doxie competes in a class for Dachshunds "eleven pounds or less at twelve months of age or older." Otherwise, all other breed standards apply.

Miniature versus Toy versus Teacup Dachshunds

A miniature Doxie weighs eleven pounds or less. Remember that the miniature Dachshund IS recognized by the American Kennel Club and is eligible for the show ring. However, the toy and teacup varieties of the Dachshund are NOT recognized by the American Kennel Club or the Dachshund Club of America.

The toy Dachshund is estimated to weigh eight pounds or less, and the only Dachshund organization that recognizes this size Doxie is the United Canine Association.

The notion of a teacup-sized pup has come with the advent of the era of the designer dog. Because these dogs are usually very small, and therefore, considered cute or unique due to their small stature, some unscrupulous dog breeders will take the smallest of the litter (these pups are often called the "runt" of the litter, and, unfortunately, they often have a lot of health problems). Some disreputable breeders will breed two runts – often multiple times – in order to keep the resulting pups quite small. Again, since many runts are plagued with health problems simply because of their size, these breeders might perpetuate health problems within these teacup pups.

Why do runts have health problems? To be frank, many times, the runt of the litter is often weaker than his siblings. He may not be able to nurse as well, which contributes to stunting in his growth, making him small. If he does not nurse properly, he may not take in all the nutrients and the ever-important immunity to certain illnesses from his mother. Then, there are illnesses or other health issues that a runt may deal with that have nothing to do with nursing. He may experience hypothermia if he happens to be pushed away from his mother. Some runts may be developmentally delayed due to malnourishment and hypothermia. In addition, some runt females used to breed as teacup moms later in life may be too small for a normal-sized litter.

Although a smaller dog is cute and somewhat desirable, be aware of the origins of a pup labeled "teacup." According to breed standards and the American Kennel Club (recognized as an authority on dog standards worldwide), there is no such thing as a teacup Dachshund, and one should be cautious when considering purchasing such.

Wire-haired Dachshund Standards

The Wire-haired Doxie sports his trademark thick outer coat that is rough to the touch and a soft undercoat which is evenly distributed throughout the coarser outer coat. The hair on a wire-haired Doxie will be smooth, much like the smooth coat Dachshund. In fact, if one sees the wire-haired Doxie distantly, he will not be able to tell the difference in a wire-haired and a smooth coat Dachshund. There should be no soft hairs in the outer coat; judges at dog shows are instructed to view this as a fault. The tail should have thick hair all over, and it should taper to a point at the end.

For the wire-haired Doxie, common colors are black and tan, wild boar, red, sable, piebald, dapple, cream (white, other than small patches of white, is not acceptable on a Doxie under any circumstances), black, chocolate, gray (which is also called blue by some enthusiasts), and fawn.

Figure 6 A wirehaired Dachshund puppy

Long-haired Dachshunds and Accepted Colors

The long-haired Doxie tends to have somewhat wavy hair. He will also have long hair on his ears (whereas other variations of the Doxie do not). Incidentally, the long-haired Dachshund will not have a uniform length of hair over the length of his body. In fact, the hair on the tail of the long-haired Dachshund is of the greatest length for this variation of the Doxie.

Like most other Dachshunds, the long-haired Doxie can be one of several colors or color patterns: black and tan, dapple, cream, red, chocolate, fawn, and more! Again, the Dachshund should only have minimal white spots on his coat to be considered acceptable.

Figure 7 A long-haired Dachshund

Typical Colors of a Dachshund:

Red Dachshund

A Dachshund with a red coat is one of the most common of the breed. A Doxie may have varying shades of red and be considered as having a red coat.

Black

A black Dachshund will have an all-black coat. He may belong to the smooth coat, wire-haired coat, or the long-haired coat group. Occasionally, he may have a spot or two of white in his otherwise dark coat.

Figure 8 A black Dachshund with a long-haired coat.

Brown

The brown Dachshund is sometimes called "fawn." The figure (Fig. 7) above depicts what is recognized as a brown Dachshund. Notice that he almost appears to have a saddle pattern on his back.

Piebald

The term "piebald" refers more to a pattern of color on a dog more than an individual color. A piebald dachshund has a white coat with patches of gray, black or brown, and he is not to be confused with a dapple-colored Doxie. A piebald Doxie will have a base color of white with red, brown, or black spots of color. Some other breeds of similar coloring might refer to this as a tri-color pattern. There are some who do refer to the piebald pattern as "spotted." Either way, the piebald pattern is not considered to be a standard color.

Figure 9 This piebald pup displays the three colors white, black, and tan.

Tan

The tan-colored Dachshund is one of the most common colors or he Doxie. He is not quite red; he is more of a brown or khaki color.

Black and Tan

Another of the most common Doxie color combinations is black and tan. Not to be confused with the piebald, the black and tan Dachshund does not sport any other color than black and tan.

Figure 10 A gorgeous black and tan adult Dachshund

Brindle

Brindle is one of the lesser common color patterns found on a Dachshund. Brindle is generally blonde or light-colored stripes on a darker base coat such as black or dark brown.

Blue

A "blue" Dachshund is also known as a gray Dachshund. It is one of the less common colorings of the Dachshund, and it is not considered to be an accepted color under the breed standards.

Dapple

The Dapple pattern (known as a "merle" pattern in some other breeds) involves a solid coat with flecks of brown and black throughout the coat. The Dapple is the only color (pattern) variation, which is allowed to have blue eyes, under the acceptable breed standards.

Figure 11 A dapple Dachshund pup

White

Although there are white Doxies, they are not considered to be an acceptable color. Cream-colored Dachshunds are, however.

Merle

Merle is the same color pattern as the dapple. It is an accepted color for the Dachshund breed standard.

Chocolate

The chocolate Doxie is often considered to be two-colored, and, under Dachshund standards, chocolate is acceptable.

Figure 12 A chocolate Doxie pup

Sable

At a distance, a sable dachshund (another rare color pattern) looks much like a black and tan dog. Looking up close however, one can observe that along the top of the dog's body, each hair is actually banded with red at the base near the skin, changing to mostly black as the strand lengthens. Sable is an accepted coat color according to breed standards.

Gray

A gray Doxie is also referred to as a "blue" Dachshund. Gray is an acceptable color according to breed standards.

Blue and Tan

The blue and tan is often bred on purpose as it is actually a dilution of the black and tan gene pool. This gene is considered recessive (therefore breeders often breed for this rare color on purpose, as it normally takes two parents possessing the recessive trait to produce the blue and tan Doxie). Although the dog is typically gray, the undertones of the gray will be blue. The dog will have the same tan points (above the eyes, on the chest, the front feet) as a black and tan Dachshund. In addition, the blue and tan Dachshund will possess a blue-colored nose, and his nails will also be a bluish color. In addition, his paw pads will be the same bluish-gray. While gray is an acceptable color, blue and tan is not on the list of acceptable colors and patterns for the Dachshund.

Spotted Dachshund

The Spotted Dachshund and the Dapple Dachshund are considered one and the same.

Other Dachshund Colors: Dapple Piebald, Isabella and Tan, Fawn, Brown Dapple, English Cream

The Dapple Piebald can be described as having larger, more uneven patch patterns. White is generally the base coat color of this Doxie, and he may have the tri-color piebald pattern in addition to some dappled spots. He may also have one brown eye and one blue eye. While this unique pattern is recognized as a Dachshund color, it is not acceptable under the breed standards.

The Isabella and Tan color pattern is closely related to chocolate and tan pattern. In fact, it is referred to as a dilution of the chocolate Dachshund. In order to definitely produce an Isabella and tan, both parents must share the Isabella/tan coloring.

A fawn-colored dog is colored much the same as an Isabella dog. They will be a light chocolate color, minus the characteristic tan markings found on the black and tan, and blue and tan Dachshund varieties. Fawn is an accepted solid color variation of the Dachshund.

Brown dapple is basically the same as a red dapple. Most breeders will tell you that the Doxie does not come in a brown color. Some may be a very dark red or have a dark red overlay (which resembles a saddle), and this might be mistaken for a brown color.

English cream (or just plain cream) is an acceptable Dachshund color, although a white Doxie is not considered to meet breed standards.

CHAPTER 4

Where Can I Buy a Dachshund?

N ow that you have determined that the Doxie is the perfect pup for you, finding a reputable breeder, or rescue, is of the utmost importance. Whether you decide to purchase a puppy or an older Dachshund, or you are considering adopting a Doxie (unfortunately, many owners are unprepared for the independence of the Dachshund and surrender their dogs to shelters), obtaining a dashing Doxie should be an enjoyable experience!

Dachshund Puppies for Sale – Finding Breeders

One must always use caution when searching for a breeder. Certainly, we have heard horror stories of puppy mills where the dogs are in ill-health, and the pups from this breeding stock are also apt to have health problems. However, this does not mean that every home breeder or backyard breeder is not to be trusted.

The American Kennel Club suggests that a reputable breeder is one who works to improve the breed. If a breeder is working to develop the breed further, then they do not need to have an elaborate breeding facility in which to raise pups for sale. However, you as the buyer should, at least, be able to visit the facilities of the breeder. The facilities should be clean, and the dogs should appear healthy. You should be able to meet at least one of the pet parents. Sometimes the breeder will have both pet parents on site; other times the mother is the only parent available. Carefully watch the parents; you can learn a lot about the possible temperament of your prospective pup by observing the mom (and dad if he is available).

It is almost too easy to jump on social media or to do a quick Internet search and look for puppy breeders. Of course, you will find a mixture of good breeders and disreputable breeders this way. Should you find a breeder online, initiate contact with the breeder and make an appointment to view the puppies.

Often, hobby breeders (those who simply love the breed and may raise one or two litters a year) do not have a large breeding operation. They may raise the pups inside their home. Do not confuse these breeders with puppy mills. Often, these breeders are just as reputable as a breeder who has invested in a large facility. This is especially true in more rural areas. Contact the breeder and set up an agreeable time to view the pups. Furthermore, trust your gut instinct. You will know by simply being around the breeder if he or she truly cares for the pups and pet parents.

How Can I Find Reputable Dachshund Breeders?

There are reputable breeders online, and the American Kennel Club offers a listing of reputable breeders associated with the AKC (these breeders are registered with the AKC and must meet certain standards in order to be recommended by the club). A detailed list of breeders can be found in the Bonus Chapter, at the end of this book.

Often reputable breeders, especially those with a larger facility, will have conducted testing to ensure that there are little to no chances that your pup will carry a genetic disease. Small-scale breeders will at least have health records on the mother showing all immunizations, vet visits, and any health issues that might be present.

Some genetic tests that you will want to look for involve the following diseases common to the Dachshund breed: IVDD (intervertebral disc disease) and PRA (progressive retinal atrophy). Often, good breeders will have a CERF (Canine Eye Registry Foundation) certificate stating that the pet parents' eyes have met the normal range of eye health. (Keep in mind that this certification is for the parent dog, not your pup. Dogs under the age of two years are not eligible for the certification testing.)

Next, observe the interaction between the pet parent and the breeder. Home breeders especially tend to treat their dogs as if the pup is a part of the family, even if they use the dog as a part of their breeding stock.

Also, notice if the breeder encourages you to contact him or her with any questions once you are ready to bring the puppy home. Does he or she offer you a card with contact information? Does he or she encourage you to keep in touch? Some breeders will even ask for pictures as the pup grows. These are all indicators that the breeder genuinely cares for the breed and is not just in the breeding business for the money.

Many times, both for your protection and their own, breeders will ask you to sign a contract. Within this contract may be a health guarantee for up to the first year of the pup's life. It should be stated here that the breeder cannot guarantee a totally healthy pup 100 percent of the time. There are things that happen which are out of the control of the breeder. For instance, illnesses such as the parvovirus can be acquired long after a pup leaves the breeder, and the breeder should not be considered responsible for this. The contract may ask you to return the dog to the breeder if you feel that you cannot properly care for the pup (as opposed to trying to give it away or sell it to a third party). Reputable breeders care about what happens to the puppies even after the dog goes to live with a new pet parent.

Ask for references from the breeder. A good breeder will have a fairly good reputation, and word of mouth is often the best testimony to a breeder's facilities.

Don't be surprised if the breeder checks you out as well! Expect him or her to ask you questions about your family, whether there are children in the home (remember, the Doxie must be handled a certain way due to his elongated spine), the ages of the children and whether you or the other members of your family have much experience with dogs. Some breeders even want to come to your home and see where the puppy will grow up. (Of course, if you live far from the breeder, this may not be possible.) Other breeders will look over your social media in order to gauge whether or not you will make a good pet parent.

One word of advice: most experts say that you should never take your puppy home without the proper papers (the pedigree). Some disreputable breeders will promise to send this documentation, but somehow never get around to it. Generally, the breeder will give you paperwork which you will fill out and send to the American Kennel Club to get your puppy registered properly. If the breeder tries to provide an excuse as to why he or she does not have this documentation, do not take the puppy home (or give the breeder the remaining balance on your pup) until you have the papers.

Reputable breeders that are registered with the AKC know that if they fail to meet certain standards to remain on the approved breeders' list that they will face other penalties, such as not being able to show their dogs at AKC-sanctioned dog shows.

Once again, trust your gut instinct when it comes to selecting a breeder! Take time to talk with the breeder. Hopefully, you will hit it off and make a good friend who will not only provide you with a healthy pup but may also become a great Doxie parent mentor to boot!

Where Can I Find Dachshunds and Dachshund Puppies (Weiner Dogs) for Sale Near Me?

A quick internet search may turn up the names of several Dachshund breeders; however, follow the guidelines listed above to ensure that you are meeting with a reputable breeder. Never send a deposit to a prospective breeder without meeting the pups and visiting the site if possible. Although it is rare, there are instances of people stealing pictures from the websites of reputable breeders and passing off the puppies as their own to scam innocent people out of money. A list of trusted breeders is included in the bonus chapter of this book.

How do I Find Long Haired Dachshund Puppies for Sale Near Me?

Again, the Internet makes searching for Dachshund pups of any kind easier than ever before! Follow the guidelines set forth by the American Kennel Club. Often, you may have to utilize word of mouth in order to find a reputable breeder. You may also contact a variety of breeders who can point you to a fellow breeder who specializes in the long-haired Doxie variety.

Is it Possible to Find a Miniature Dachshund for Sale?

Yes! Miniature Dachshunds are recognized as an acceptable variation of the Dachshund breed, and you may be able to utilize the Internet to find Mini Doxie breeders in your area. Remember always to follow the guidelines set forth previously in this chapter for selecting a breeder. Also, when you visit, observe the pups and their parents. You want to see healthy pups that are not too shy. You also want to see a breeder interact in a healthy way with the pups and any adult Doxies present.

What is the Average Miniature Dachshund Price?

A standard Dachshund with papers generally costs between $300 - $600. You can expect a Miniature Dachshund to cost more than a standard Doxie; prices will vary among breeders and will also depend upon your location.

How Do I Find Reputable Miniature Dachshund Breeders?

Finding a reputable Miniature Dachshund breeder is much like searching for a standard Doxie reputable breeder. The American Kennel Club has a listing of approved (registered) breeders via their website (a list will also be included at the end of this book as well). Prospective buyers are also advised to attend dog shows in their area. Here you can meet people who love the breed, and they can point you in the direction of reputable breeders near you.

How About Standard Dachshunds and Standard Dachshund Puppies for Sale?

Doxies are one of the most popular breeds today, so finding a breeder who specializes in Standard-sized Doxies should be no problem. You will want to visit the breeder's facilities and observe the breeder, the pups, and their parents.

You might be faced with a situation in which you might need to ship a pup. This might take place when there are no breeders in your area and driving to the breeder's facilities is out of the question. I would suggest using only those breeders registered with either the American Kennel Club or the Dachshund Club of America. You can rest assured that any breeder registered with either of these organizations has been vetted by the club. If you need to ship a pup, be prepared to include that in the purchase price. Shipping depends upon location and may add an extra $200 - $400 to your final purchase price.

Where Can I Find Wire-haired Dachshund Breeders?

Trusted resources such as the breeders registered through the Dachshund Club of American and the American Kennel Club. In addition, your veterinarian may also be able to recommend a breeder you can trust. Don't have a veterinarian yet? Ask some friends about their vet and get some recommendations via word of mouth.

Where Can I Find Cream Dachshund Puppies or Piebald Patterned Puppies for Sale?

The cream-colored Dachshund and those with a piebald pattern are relatively easy to find. You may need to speak with those who breed standard Dachshunds in order to get the names and contact information of breeders who specialize in the more elusive piebald pattern. Cream-colored pups might be a little easier to find but finding a trusted breeder who can point you to other breeders likely to have a pup of this color will ensure that you get a quality dog.

How Difficult is it to Find Dapple Dachshund Puppies for Sale?

Certainly, dapple Dachshunds are rarer than their solid-coated peers, but they are not always easy to find. A quick Internet search will net you some potential names of breeders, but you will need to keep in mind the guidelines for discerning whether or not a person is a reputable breeder. A recommendation from a trusted friend or a veterinarian will go a long way in helping you find a dapple Doxie pup.

CHAPTER 5

Should I Consider Adopting a Dachshund?

S o, you want a Dachshund, and you are perfectly happy with an older dog/ Consider adopting an adolescent or older Doxie!

How Do I Find a Dachshund Rescue or Dachshunds for Adoption Near Me?

Dachshund rescue organizations are common across the United States and many countries. If there is not a Doxie rescue in your area, it is almost certain that there will be another in a neighboring state or area.

Because rescues deal with animals who have been neglected or abandoned, you can be sure that those working for the organization will ensure that you are a good match for your new Doxie. Your adopted Dachshund will have been spayed or neutered, and, should he be experiencing any health issues when surrendered to the shelter, he should be receiving any necessary medical treatments.

The All-American Dachshund Rescue is located in the Southeastern United States, but the organization places surrendered or rescued Doxies all over North America. It is only one of many Dachshund rescues across the United States.

How Difficult is it to Find Dachshund Puppies for Adoption?

Unfortunately, because Doxies can be stubborn and are not easy to housebreak, many young Dachshunds are surrendered to shelters. In fact, many Dachshund shelters will insist that potential adoptive Doxie parents educate themselves on Dachshund behavior. While Dachshunds are wonderful dogs, and many Doxie parents claim they will never have another breed, those without much experience when it comes to canines may not have the patience required to train a Dachshund properly. They give up, and the dog may end up surrendered to a shelter. The goal of the shelter is to ensure that surrendered pups and/ or rescues go to a forever home that will be beneficial to both the new pet parents and the dog itself.

Where Can I Find a Miniature Dachshund Rescue or Mini Dachshunds for Adoption?

The Dachshund Club of America and The Kennel Club in the United Kingdom list rescues in America and in the UK, where Miniature Dachshunds can be found awaiting their forever homes. Of course, it never hurts to check with standard Dachshund rescues, when searching for a Miniature Dachshund.

Are there Rescues Devoted Specifically to Dapple Dachshund Rescue Dogs?

No. However, check with standard Dachshund rescues to find dapple and miniature Dachshunds. You just might find your perfect pup waiting at a Dachshund rescue.

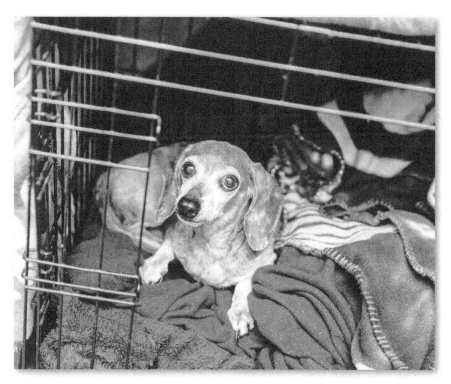

Figure 13 Rescues are a great way to give a Dachshund a better life.

Is there such a Thing as a Dachshund Sanctuary? Is it Possible to Adopt from One?

Yes. One, in particular, is The Promised Land Dachshund Sanctuary https://thepromisedlanddachshundsanctuary.org/ , which takes in Dachshunds, but is also open to other breeds such as Chihuahuas and German Shepherds. Often, the dogs who end up in the Sanctuary have health issues. Each dog will be spayed or neutered. In theory, the dogs housed by The Promised Land Dachshund Sanctuary could be adopted, but because many of the dogs living in the Sanctuary have health issues, finding homes for the pups proves difficult.

The Dachshund Club of America lists shelters that specialize in Dachshunds. One can also consult the National Dachshund Rescue List in order to find a Dachshund Rescue organization or a Dachshund sanctuary in the area. A list of links to rescues can be found at the end of this book.

Figure 14 The Dachshund requires little in the way of maintenance

CHAPTER 6

What Items Will I Need in Order to Care for my Dachshund?

Congratulations on the acquisition of your new best buddy! Dachshund owners declare that they will never own any other type of breed after living with a Doxie. The Dachshund has a personality all its own, and his penchant for silly antics juxtaposed with lots of cuddles makes the Dachshund owner love him all the more! Whether you are bringing your new fur baby home soon, or he is getting settled in, a few purchases are in order to ensure that your new pooch is happy and healthy.

What Type of Dog Food is Best for my Dachshund?

In sharing this information, my goal is not to promote one brand name of dog food over another. In fact, I would like to give you a good deal of information and tips, so that you can find the most nutritional food for your dog.

Keep in mind that Dachshunds tend to gain weight, particularly if they do not receive proper exercise. One way to combat this is to make sure that there are not excess fats in your Doxie's dog food.

First, when choosing a proper, nutritionally balanced food for your Dachshund, one must learn to read labels carefully. Also, keep in mind that the most expensive foods are not always the best foods for your dog. Personally, I have bought some of the most expensive brands – the ones that promised to be all-natural and totally nutritious – and my dogs refused to eat it! You may find yourself experimenting with a variety of foods before finding the best one for your dog.

Now, let's discuss what you should look for when reading the label of dog food. Look for the terms "balanced" and "AAFCO approved." These are positive things that you WANT to see on the label. Next, look for ingredients to AVOID on the food bag: meal by-products, meat by-products, certain color additives, BHA, BHT, Ethoxyquin, and Propylene Glycol. In addition, you want to ensure that your dog's food label reads "pet grade," quality rather than "feed grade."

Let's look more closely at what each of these harmful ingredients is, and the possible negative effects of ingesting these unhealthy items on a regular basis. First, meal by-products are generally considered "fillers" in dog food. Meat by-products are used much the same way. To be honest, meat and meal by-products are derived by grinding up leftover animal parts (the parts left over after slaughter – bones, intestines, even chicken feathers that cannot otherwise be disposed of). Again, these are fillers, and they are often used to add flavor to dry dog food. Generally, if you see meat or meal by-product at the beginning of a list of ingredients, avoid that dog food.

Next, look for any color additives, particularly Blue 2, Red 40, Yellow 5 and 6. These colors are especially harmful to dogs. Color additives have been linked to allergic reactions and cancer in animals. Sadly, there is absolutely no reason to add food color to dog food. The color is only added to make the food look more appealing to a dog's owners, not the dog – who sees no colors!

Two of the most harmful chemicals that can be added to your pup's dry dog food are BHA and BHT. BHA is an acronym for Butylated Hydroxyanisole. It is a chemical preservative that is found in a lot of commercial dog foods as well as treats. BHA is a known carcinogen, as is BHT (Butylated Hydroxytoluene), also a chemical preservative. (In addition, look for the chemical preservative Ethoxyquin. It should also be avoided at all costs.) Each of these chemicals has been proven to cause cancer in lab rats.

*It should be noted that the term "Ethoxyquin" is not often found on a food label. It will be presented as "fish meal."

By law, a food label cannot make false claims. This is true whether the food label is present on human food, or on a bag of pet food. Therefore, a statement claiming "no artificial preservatives" on your dog's food label guarantees that none of the abovementioned harmful chemicals can be found in the dog food.

Propylene Glycol is a moistening agent present in many solid dog foods. Unfortunately, Propylene Glycol is a derivative of anti-freeze, which is highly toxic to dogs.

Now that you know what ingredients to avoid when choosing a dog food, what ingredients SHOULD we want to find on the food label? Vitamins such as A, B, C, D, E, and K should be a part of the food you choose for your Dachshund. Also, look for the claim "Made in the USA" somewhere on the dog food bag. This guarantees that the food has been prepared according to FDA standards for pet food.

Another consideration is choosing wet dog food versus dry kibble. Wet dog food contains more moisture than dry dog food, which can be beneficial if your dog does not drink a lot of water. In addition, canned (wet) dog food contains almost all proteins with little carbohydrates. Wet dog food rarely contains the artificial preservatives that are often present in dry kibble. The can is sealed; therefore, you need not worry about the harmful chemicals BHT and BHA or Ethoxyquin being present in your canned (wet) dog food.

As a bonus, wet dog food is generally more appealing to your dog, as compared to dry kibble. Experts tell us that even picky eaters are likely to eat canned dog food when they will eat nothing else. Furthermore, wet dog food is often a better choice for smaller dogs such as the Dachshund.

Finally, dry dog food often contains the fillers, preservatives, and other potentially harmful chemicals because the manufacturer is attempting to make it more palatable to the dog. To be sure, you may spend a little more to give your dog wet (canned) dog food, but, in the end, you must decide which type of food is most beneficial for your pup.

In the interest of making sure that your Doxie does not gain too much weight, I am including a chart of the proper amount of food your Dachshund should take in, on a daily basis.

Feeding Quantities for an Average Dachshund

	¾ cup	1 cup	1 ½ cup	2 Cups
Toy	X			
Miniature	X			
Small Standard (17 – 20 pounds)		X		
Medium Standard (20 – 25 pounds)			X	
Large Standard (26 – 32 pounds)				X

Should I Make My Own Dachshund Dog Food?

Personally, I am a huge fan of cooking your dog's food. This ensures that your pup is getting the proper nutrition without having to rely on commercially-made dog food to nourish your fur baby. However, not everyone has the time to prepare the proper amount of food for his or her dog. Plus, if you have multiple dogs, you will need to prepare twice the amount of food, which can be tricky if you have no experience in this.

Should you choose to cook your dog's food, you will need to ensure that there are no preservatives or chemicals in the food that you prepare. Meat should be the primary ingredient in your home-made dog food. Chicken, fish, lamb, and beef are all great initial ingredients for your home-made dog meals. Each of these meats is high in protein. Be sure to look for meats that are organic (this ensures that no antibiotics have been used to treat the animals prior to processing). Also, the AAFCO approves rice, peas or carrots, and sweet potatoes. Some brands may use pumpkin as an alternative healthy carbohydrate. These items can be purchased at your local market and prepared in your own kitchen for roughly the same price as a sixteen-pound bag of dry kibble.

First, choose the type of meat that you wish to prepare. It is always a good idea to give your pup a variety of meats so that he does not become burned out on a particular food. Beef – particularly stew meat or beef tips as well as stir-fry beef – is a great alternative to chicken or lamb. It is also equally healthy for your Doxie! I do not recommend ground beef or ground chuck, however. This cut of meat is often rather greasy, which can cause stomach upset in your pup.

Whatever meat you choose, boil the meat using a minimum amount of salt (I prefer sea salt as it packs a lot of flavor in a small amount). White rice is considered a "novel" grain – this means that white rice does not have the potential to evoke an allergic reaction like other grains, such as corn, might. To make things easier, you can add canned carrots (organic, of course) and peas. Diced potatoes and green beans are also good for your pup. Depending upon the amount of rice you cook, this amount of food (roughly three pounds of meat, four cups of rice, and the vegetables) will yield a week's worth of food for slightly less than a bag of dry kibble. In addition, you will be assured of exactly what ingredients are present in your dog's food. Plus, your pup will be so excited to eat "human" food that he is unlikely to turn your freshly prepared meal away!

I have been feeding my own dogs this type of diet and, I have noticed in my own pups so many benefits. Of course, you may not be able to make your dog's meals. That does not make you any less of a pet parent! Just remember to read food labels and weed out any unhealthy food choices.

How Can I Be Sure I Have Purchased Healthy Dog Treats for my Dachshund?

Using treats in training your Doxie is most necessary, so purchasing healthy treats for your pup is also important. Like dog food, dog treats can be cheaply made. However, if you will look at the ingredients, you can be assured that you are purchasing a quality product for your pup.

First, a treat for your Doxie should be relatively low-calorie. Remember, the Dachshund has a tendency to gain weight, so a small treat with relatively few calories (some treats only have ten to twenty calories per treat; this is what you want to find). Experts recommend that no more than seventy calories come from a dog's treats, so keep this in mind when choosing a treat for your Doxie. Treats should be soft and tasty. Look for treats that are made with real meat (labels will boast of this). Be sure that the treats contain no BHA, BHT or Ethoxyquin – look for the term "no artificial preservatives" on the label. Also, look for "Made in the USA" on the bag, which will assure you that the treats meet FDA standards.

The most important thing to remember when purchasing treats is this: small, tasty, and soft treats with no artificial preservatives or additives. Your Doxie will thank you for it!

What Should I Look for When Purchasing a Dog Bed for my Dachshund?

Doxies allowed to sleep with their humans will often snuggle down into the covers. Therefore, you will want to keep this in mind when purchasing a dog bed for your pup. The Dachshund likes to be snug and warm. In addition, getting your Doxie to rest in a dog bed rather than your bed will prevent him from jumping from the bed and possibly injuring his distinctive spine. (NOTE: If you do allow your Dachshund to sleep with you in your bed, it might be a good investment to purchase puppy stairs so that your pup will not be tempted to jump down to the floor from your bed.)

A proper dog bed should provide your Dachshund with comfort, warmth, a sense of security, and provide him with a space of his own. Consider how your Doxie likes to sleep. If he prefers to stretch out, then you will need to ensure that the bed is long enough for him to do so. Experts recommend measuring your pup, then adding from six to ten inches to the dog's length – this is the size dog bed you should purchase. If you notice that he likes to snuggle in the covers, then covered beds are a good idea for your Doxie. If you notice that your pup tends to curl up to sleep, then a dog bed described as a "donut" bed may be appropriate for your Dachshund. An oval-shaped bed is also a good option for the Doxie, regardless of his sleep position.

If you are investing in an older dog that might be arthritic, you can invest in a raised bed which takes pressure off the body of your dog. Raised beds are also a good choice for areas that experience regularly high temperatures (the American South or the Southwest) – cooler air can circulate beneath the raised bed and keep your pooch cool.

Certainly, you can always add covers to your dog's bed, and, as your Doxie ages, you may consider adding orthopedic pads to his bedding. This will simply add cushioning to his bedding and keep him comfortable.

What is the Best Type of Dachshund Puppy Food?

Puppies need special nutrition to be certain. In fact, choosing the proper food for your Dachshund puppy is just as important as selecting nutritious food for your adult dog.

The first twelve months of any dog's life are paramount to the dog's overall health as an adult dog. In order to grow into healthy adult dogs, the Dachshund pup will need just the right amount of vitamins, minerals, and other nutrients.

You will want to scan the ingredient label of a variety of dog foods in order to select healthy food for your Doxie baby. You will want to avoid artificial preservatives and colors just as you would with adult dog food. Remember that the term "meal or meat by-product" is to be avoided. Another term that you should look for (and avoid) is animal by-products. Animal by-products are what is left of an animal that has been slaughtered for food. This could be anything from the carcass that is not normally processed for human food, such as the lips, intestines, and bones. Any time you see "by-product" on a pet food product, remember that these are not true meats. Furthermore, if you see any "by-product" ingredient at the top of a food label, put that product back and looks for a healthier alternative. These products are never healthy for your pup no matter how young or old he is!

Now that we have discovered what should not be in your pup's food let's focus on the things that one should expect to see in nutritious puppy food.

Look for ingredients which promote healthy brain development. DHA omega fatty acids are key to developing the young brain, and many commercially made brands of puppy food contain this ingredient. In addition, look for probiotics as an ingredient in puppy food. This will help to build a better digestive system in your pup. NOTE: Dachshunds are sometimes prone to GDV (Gastric Dilation Volvulus), also known as bloat. Building a healthy immune system from the time your pup is young may help to prevent this often-fatal illness.

Puppy food should also be formulated to contain a higher level of protein compared to adult dog food, and they often have more carbohydrates (which is converted to energy for the young pup). It is important to provide your young puppy with a higher amount of protein and carbohydrates so that he will grow properly. Some pet parents do not comprehend that the specially formulated puppy food is truly better for your pup at a young age. However, if you will commit to feeding your puppy only puppy food during his first year, you will be contributing to his overall good health as an adult Doxie.

Other important ingredients a puppy food must provide include: L-carnitine, EPA omega-3 fatty acids, fiber, and whole grains. Fiber and probiotics promote digestive health. EPA omega-3 fatty acids and L-carnitine aid in the development of healthy coats and eyes.

Earlier, the topic of cooking a healthy meal for your adult Doxie was discussed. To be truthful, unless you can prepare a meal that includes these important minerals and nutrients, I recommend choosing a puppy food that includes – at a minimum – DHA fatty acids for brain development, probiotics, and a high amount of protein and healthy carbohydrates (whole grains). You should feed this to your pup for at least the first year of life to ensure he obtains all the benefits these special minerals provide.

Figure 15 The Dachshund has a healthy appetite

Harness vs. Dachshund Dog Collar

Particular care must be taken when choosing a harness and/or collar for the Dachshund. Regular harnesses will not fit the Doxie properly, so you should take your dog's measurements in order to ensure just the right fit.

When looking for a harness for your Dachshund, you will need to consider the chest strap, the neck measurement, and the girth of the harness.

First, measure the girth (the area just above the ribcage) of your Doxie. The harness will need to be at least an inch more in circumference than your Doxie's actual girth. Then, measure the length between the neck and the girth area (this is where the chest strap will sit). Finally, you will need to measure the size of your Dachshund's neck. In order for your Doxie to be comfortable while wearing his harness, you will need to have correct measurements, particularly in his chest area.

When choosing a harness, consider the number of adjustment points available on the item. Experts recommend at least four adjustment points.

Measuring Your Doxie

For the girth: Place a cloth tape measure (such as one that would be used by a seamstress or tailor) about one to two inches behind your dog's front legs. Holding this end of the measuring tape steady, wrap the tape around your dog's ribcage.

For the chest strap: You will want to put the tape measure at a comfortable place below the dog's throat – too close to the throat and he will feel a choking sensation; too far down the chest and the harness will be ill-fitting and perhaps chafe your pup. Stretch the tape to the area where you measured for the girth (about one or two inches behind his front legs). Wrap the tape around one of the front legs, then stretch the tape about one or two inches on the other side of the remaining front leg.

For the neck: Wrap the measuring tape around the base of your dog's neck (the thickest area). This will be the circumference of your dog's neck.

Is a harness better than a collar? Experts say yes. The Doxie is often prone to issues with his neck and vertebrae. Using a collar puts pressure on the neck, which is not healthy for the Dachshund. A harness puts pressure on the powerful chest area of the Dachshund rather than his much more vulnerable neck. So, in order to promote good spinal health in your Doxie, use a properly fitting harness when taking him for a stroll outdoors.

What are Top Recommendations for a Dachshund Dog Leash?

When considering a leash, choose a leash that is at least four to six feet in length. It is my personal experience that nylon is durable and also cost-friendly. While leather leashes are just as durable as the nylon variety, leashes made from cotton or rubber are more likely to break.

There are other types of leashes available to you, such as the retractable leash and the hands-free leash (for those who enjoy taking a run with their pups). I do not recommend the retractable leash for use with the powerful Dachshund. Should he decide to pull, the leash can come undone with the right amount of pressure. Where hands-free leashes are concerned, no one brand is better than another. Stick with nylon for the durability it provides.

Remember, your Doxie should always be leashed when outdoors (unless he is inside a fenced-in area, of course). The prey drive is strong with a Dachshund, and they tend to chase cats, squirrels, and other small animals. No matter how well trained your Doxie is, his prey drive is stronger! In order to avoid any trouble, it is wiser to simply keep him leashed.

What are the Best Dachshund Dog Toys?

Simply put, toys which allow the Doxie to play out what comes to him naturally are the best for him. The Dachshund was trained to burrow into holes after his prey. Experts recommend chew toys which allow for treats to be stuffed inside them. The Doxie will enjoy working toward the "prey" inside the chew toy. The Dachshund generally works in short bursts of speed; however, the Doxie is not a dog who enjoys games of fetch. He does, however, enjoy playing with small balls (he will nuzzle and chase the ball).

Some owners even play a Doxie version of hide and seek! They place toys throughout the home as a "prize" for the Dachshund to find. Again, this serves to allow for play in the instinctual strengths of the Doxie. This will stimulate the Dachshund's mind as well as give him physical activity.

Are there any toys you should avoid when owning a Dachshund? Unfortunately, yes! If you purchase toys with squeakers inside, be prepared to clean up the stuffing so often found within this type of dog toy. Dachshunds will enthusiastically tear open a soft toy in search of the pesky squeaker! Further, these could present choking hazards.

Will I Need to Purchase a Dachshund House?

First, Dachshunds are small dogs that thrive on companionship. They should live inside the home primarily. However, dog experts and Doxie owners alike suggest that you provide a fenced-in area for your Dachshund. Should you decide to leave the Dachshund in this area for more than an hour daily, and, if you live in an area where temperatures are very high during the summer (the American South or Southwest) or perhaps your yard does not have much in the way of trees, you may consider purchasing a dog house for your Doxie.

Although your Doxie will not spend the majority of his time in an outdoor dog house, you will still want to ensure that he is comfortable when he does utilize the house. An ideal dog house will be big enough for your dog to walk inside of, turn around, and lie down comfortably. Measure your dog from nose to the base of the tail. In addition, measure his height (because the Doxie is so low to the ground, height really shouldn't be an issue). Generally, a Dachshund is comfortable in a dog house considered "extra small."

Dachshund Carriers and Dog Crates

Planning to travel with your Doxie? You will most definitely need a dog carrier! The elongated body of the Dachshund can be difficult to fit into just any old carrier, and, because the Doxie does tend to suffer from spinal issues, you will want to protect him by purchasing a carrier for travel.

The perfect carrier for your Doxie is much like the perfect dog house – your Dachshund will need to be able to stand up, turn around, and lay down inside of the carrier. A carrier that is too big may cause your pup to slide during transport (which might not injure him but could lead to anxiety). The type of dog carrier is not nearly as important as the fact that your Doxie has ample room inside of the carrier. Some pet parents prefer a hard-plastic carrier (you can always place a soft blanket inside; plus, the plastic carrier provides more protection than a soft-sided carrier). Other Doxie parents prefer the soft-sided carrier, claiming that the dog has more room to make adjustments. Either of these is safe for your pet; this will simply be a decision that you should make based on your preference.

I am a firm believer in crating dogs from an early age. Now, dogs absolutely can NOT stay inside a crate at all times, but, as a pet parent who has dealt with dogs with separation anxiety, a crate can be a lifesaver! More information on crates and crate training is forthcoming.

Figure 16 A soft dog carrier provides safe travels for your Doxie

Dachshund Pet Gates – Are they Necessary?

This is another item which is really only necessary if you deem it so. Pet gates are needed only if you have a room in which the Doxie is not allowed, or if there is a room in which you wish to keep the Doxie from leaving. For instance, you may want to keep your dog in the utility room when you are away from home. A pet gate is a great tool for keeping the dog in an enclosure, but, at the same time, your dog will be able to see through the gate (most have a diamond-shaped pattern that is see-through). Again, this is a personal decision and not a necessary item.

Will my Dachshund Need Supplements or Vitamins?

While your Dachshund does not necessarily need supplements, in order to help him live a long and healthy life, you will want to give your Doxie supplements that will help keep him healthy.

Because the Dachshund tends to have joint problems, supplements such as glucosamine and chondroitin have proven to ease joint pain in older Doxies. This supplement can be found in a chewable form to aid in ease of administration. This is the most common form of supplement given to Dachshunds.

Some Dachshund parents will also give their pooch supplements which help the coat stay sleek and shiny, and others give their pups probiotics or other digestive aids. Giving your pup these supplements is strictly the decision of the pet parent.

What Items will I Need to Keep My Dachshund Clean: Shampoo, Brush, other Care Items

The Dachshund is special in that there are three coat types. This will determine many items you will need to keep your Doxie looking clean and healthy. We will begin with the smooth-coat Dachshund and his needs.

Experts recommend bathing the Dachshund only when necessary. When it is time for a good bath, be careful that the shampoo you choose is safe for your Dachshund. The best shampoo for all dogs is an all-natural one. Keep in mind that many manufacturers will label a product "all-natural," yet there are tons of additives in the shampoo! In order to meet the "all-natural" standard, only a few ingredients need be present in order for manufacturers to claim the product is natural. For most dog product manufacturers, the terms "organic" and "all-natural" are simply marketing tools. Unfortunately, the general public is rarely able to tell the difference. However, a few tips will help you decipher the mystery of the ingredient label.

First, look for terms such as "proprietary blend" and "naturally derived." Products with these terms are most definitely not all-natural! In fact, this often signifies that the manufacturer only added a few truly natural ingredients, or perhaps the natural ingredients in the product are extremely watered down.

Second, you should look at the product itself. If the shampoo is thick or a bright color, then you can bet the product is not all natural. If the product is thick, it is likely that additives have been introduced to the natural product. Furthermore, bright

colors such as pink or blue – as well as a strong fragrance –
are indicative that the product is not natural. Dog shampoo
manufacturers often add ingredients to their products in
order to make it appear the same as the shampoo humans use;
these ingredients can be rather irritating to your dog's skin. In
addition, bright colors are added to make dog shampoo more
appealing to our human tastes. Again, this is harmful to your
dog and should be avoided. Truly natural dog shampoos look
and have the consistency of cooking oil – a thin consistency and
slightly yellow color.

An all-natural dog shampoo should be only lightly fragranced
(if at all). Often, manufacturers will add a multitude of harmful
chemicals to a dog shampoo in order to give it some fragrance.
These chemicals can severely irritate your dog's sensitive skin and
may possibly cause hair loss over a period of time.

By law, a manufacturer is not compelled to list all the ingredients
on dog shampoo. You may simply see terms such as "fragrance"
and "natural colorants" – but don't be fooled! In an all-natural
product, you should see none of these terms on the label, and the
product should pass the consistency and smell test as well.

To be sure, the only real way to know that you are purchasing a
safe shampoo is to look for the phrase "certified organic" on the
ingredient label. Remember, manufacturers are not allowed to
make unsubstantiated claims, so, if shampoo is labeled USDA
Certified Organic, you can believe that it is so. In order to
receive this label, a product must meet certain guidelines, and
artificial fragrances and colors are not allowed in these products.
To be certain, you will likely spend more for a certified organic

shampoo, but you are saving money by preventing skin issues and other health problems likely to come about when using cheaply made products containing chemicals.

(NOTE: The above advice on dog shampoo goes with any Dachshund coat type.)

When choosing a brush for your Dachshund, a natural, bristle-type brush is often best for the short-haired Doxie. This soft brush will not irritate the skin of your Dachshund, and it will promote the release of natural oils in the Doxie's skin.

The wire-haired Doxie also requires a soft-bristle brush. You should brush a wire-haired Dachshund at least three times a week. Wire-haired Dachshunds also need to be combed after a brushing. This will remove any dead hair and debris from the coat. A fine-toothed comb will suffice for this.

Wire-haired Doxies should be "stripped" twice a year – once during the spring and again in the fall (typically times when dogs shed the most). Stripping is much like brushing the coat; only you will go in the opposite direction of the growth. You will also need to use a pin brush to strip the coat.

A long-haired Dachshund will also need to be brushed at least three times a week. A pin brush should be purchased to brush the long-haired Doxie.

What Other Items will I Need to Purchase Before Bringing my Dachshund Home (Dachshund Dog Bowls, Kennels, Products, and Accessories)?

Certainly, you will need everyday items such as food and watering bowls, nail clippers, and toys. Any kind of food bowl will do as long as it is heavy enough that your Doxie doesn't knock it over during meal time. From personal experience, when purchasing a watering bowl, I really like the automatic water bowl. It is especially good for those of us with busy lifestyles. It works much like the large water bottles you might find in an office. The water bottle is filled and turned upside down, and, as your dog empties the water bowl, water in the bottle will refill the bowl. It is also heavy enough that you will not likely deal with your pup knocking it over.

You may want to purchase a toothbrush and toothpaste for your Dachshund. This promotes good dental health in your pup. You should begin brushing his teeth on a regular basis when your pup is small so that he becomes used to the routine.

You will also need nail clippers for your Doxie. This is another part of the grooming routine that should be adopted as soon as possible. The sooner a pup gets used to the grooming routine; the easier life will be for you.

Dachshund Dog Crate

I once thought that crating a dog was a little too much like putting them in a cage. However, one of my dogs suffers from separation anxiety, and the crate is her saving grace! I have also used the crate to aid in potty training. The crate, for me, is imperative when owning a dog! Now, with that said, one should NEVER leave a dog in the crate for long periods of time, especially if you are at home. It is perfectly fine to leave the dog inside the crate while you are at work, provided that he has access to water, but leaving a dog crated both day and night is cruel, particularly when all your pup really wants is to spend time with you.

Speaking of using a crate to combat separation anxiety, you should train your Doxie so that the crate becomes a safe space for him. Start your pup at a young age. Place a trail of treats in the crate. Once he goes inside, shut the door. Allow him to see you leaving. Get out of his sight for only five minutes at a time, working up to ten minutes. He may whine at first, and you should fight the instinct to take him out right away (you will teach him that all he needs to do is whine when something unpleasant happens, and he will be removed from the situation). Try to leave him in his crate for at least five minutes without his whining. Then, when you return, make a "big deal" out of the event (greet him, act excited as if you've been gone from him for some time). Slowly extend this time to ten minutes. In addition, place a favorite blanket and a toy along with water in his crate. After a while, you will no longer need to use treats to entice him into the crate. He will go willingly.

Because the Dachshund is not a large dog, you will likely be able to purchase a medium-sized crate for your pup. This size crate is usually 30 in x 19 in x 21 in (76.2 cm x 48.26 cm x 53.34 cm). It is often the perfect size for a Dachshund.

Figure 17 A wire crate

CHAPTER 7

What Should I Consider When Purchasing a Dachshund?

What Vaccinations can I Expect my Dachshund Puppy to Receive?

The exact vaccinations your Dachshund will be required to receive by law may vary from state to state. At six weeks, your puppy will receive his first round of immunizations. Generally, this set of shots is administered while your pup is still in the care of the breeder. Be sure to ask for shot records if they are not attached to your sales contract.

The first (six weeks) set of immunizations will likely include protection against distemper, kennel cough (also known as "bordetella," a highly contagious respiratory disease among canines), and parvovirus. This set of immunization occurs while the puppy is still with the breeder.

At twelve weeks (likely the first set of immunizations that you will need to provide for your pup), the veterinarian will administer a second dose of prevention against distemper, parvovirus, and bordetella. A vaccination for infectious hepatitis will be administered at this time.

At fourteen weeks, you will once again return to the vet for a third booster of the distemper vaccination. A third parvovirus booster shot will be administered as well at this time. The second booster for infectious hepatitis will be included in the immunization schedule also.

At this visit, you may also be asked about whether or not you'd like to immunize your pup against Lyme disease and leptospirosis.

At sixteen weeks, the final round of shots for your pup's first year will be administered. Parvovirus and rabies immunizations are required at this time, with the option to add booster shots for Lyme disease and leptospirosis.

When your Dachshund reaches one year of age, you will return for one final round of booster shots. This includes a final parvovirus immunization as well as a final dose of the distemper and infectious hepatitis booster. A final dosage against rabies will be administered as well. Pet parents will also be given the option to administer the bordetella immunization a final time, as well as a parainfluenza, leptospirosis, and Lyme vaccination.

Schedule of vaccinations through the first year

AVERAGE AGE AT VACCINE ADMINISTRATION	VACCINES ADMINISTERED
Six Weeks	Distemper Bordetella Parvovirus
Twelve Weeks	Distemper Bordetella Parvovirus Infectious Hepatitis
Fourteen Weeks	Parvovirus booster Distemper booster Infectious hepatitis *Lyme disease * Leptospirosis *This denotes these are optional vaccinations.
Sixteen Weeks	Parvovirus booster Rabies *Lyme disease *Leptospirosis *This denotes that these are optional vaccinations.
One Year	Boosters for all previous vaccinations

Is the Dachshund Good with Kids?

Certainly! Remember that the Dachshund lives best with older children. However, should children come along after your Doxie has been a part of the family for some time, then simply put some effort into teaching the children how to pick up a Dachshund properly. Always remember that the Doxie spine is prone to issues that can be avoided if the Dachshund is carried properly.

Generally, the Dachshund loves playing with children. He has a lot of energy, and children usually keep him occupied with lots of play. The Dachshund is quite patient with children and finds them to be wonderful playmates.

Figure 18 The Dachshund makes a great playmate for children

Does the Dachshund Experience any Health Issues?

Oftentimes, your Dachshund will live a long, healthy life. However, one would be remiss without sharing possible health issues that a Doxie may experience during his lifetime.

Throughout the book, I have made mention of the elongated body of the Dachshund and the need for him to refrain from jumping from heights. I've also made mention of carrying the Doxie properly so as not to injure his spine. This is due to the fact that the Dachshund's top potential health issue is Intervertebral Disc Disease or IVDD. Even if your pup's parents are in the best of health, this genetic illness can pop up in otherwise healthy dogs. (In other words, there is no genetic test that can assure you that your pup will never acquire IVDD.) With IVDD, the vertebrae weaken and, in some cases, protrude into the spinal canal. Often, IVDD is caused by spinal stress, and, can be somewhat prevented. Precautionary steps include: helping your dog maintain a healthy weight throughout his life, keeping your dog from jumping from furniture or your bed, and keeping his spine horizontal should you need to carry him. Again, one cannot completely prevent IVDD, but using these precautions may help minimize the risk.

Second, many Dachshunds experience patellar luxation, which is basically a dislocation of the kneecap from its proper position. Some experts refer to this as loose knees. The very short legs of the Dachshunds make them somewhat prone to patellar luxation. A Doxie with this issue may limp along to relieve pressure on the affected leg. Again, keeping your Dachshund at a healthy weight will go a long way in preventing this condition.

Doxies are also prone to hip dysplasia, which is characterized by the thigh bone being deformed and unable to fit properly into the hip socket. Symptoms are much like those with patellar luxation. You will notice the Doxie limping or favoring one leg to compensate for the pain.

Next, some Dachshunds experience issues with eye health. Dry eyes, Progressive Retinal Atrophy (PRA), and cataracts are common eye problems the Doxie may deal with. PRA is a degenerative disease that can lead to blindness. There is no treatment for PRA. Cataracts in dogs are much like cataracts in humans, and they can be corrected with surgery.

Some Dachshunds are also affected by deafness.

Figure 19 Regular veterinarian visits will ensure a long, healthy life for your Doxie

What Makes the Dachshund Muzzle Special?

The Dachshund has a sharply keen nose, and, unfortunately, he is often controlled by it! It is pointless to hide treats or food from the Dachshund – he can literally sniff it out! Although the Dachshund is a small dog, he is a hound – particularly, he is a scent hound. His long muzzle only aids in his ability to scent prey.

Figure 20 The Dachshund is a powerful digger

CHAPTER 8

What is Involved in Breeding and Raising Dachshunds?

F irst, let me say that I personally advocate spaying and neutering pets. There are many health benefits that accompany this type of surgery. Dogs that have been altered tend to live longer than those who are left intact. Certain cancers can be avoided if a dog is spayed or neutered; in addition, you can prevent reproductive issues. However, there are benefits to breeding dogs as well. Just as a precaution, however, I do recommend spaying or neutering your pup after one or two litters to promote their overall health.

Breeding Dachshunds – just like when you are breeding any breed of dog – requires a great commitment on the part of the breeder. As stated previously in the book, those who breed should seek to improve the quality of the breed in their endeavors. You can expect to invest a great deal of time, and often money, to breed Dachshunds. However, the reward for finding suitable homes for your sweet pups is often well worth the investment you put into breeding Doxies.

First, attend dog shows. Get acquainted with experienced breeders. They will serve as mentors and can be a wealth of knowledge on your journey into raising Doxie pups. Feel free to ask them about the pros and cons of breeding. Once you have established a good rapport with an experienced breeder, hopefully, he or she will be a resource you can tap for years to come.

First, you should allow your female to experience at least two "seasons" or "heats" before attempting to breed her. This will ensure that she is fully matured and that she has built up the proper amount of nutrients in her body in order to handle the stress of carrying pups.

Next, you will need to prepare your Dachshund dam for pregnancy. She will need to be wormed, and she should have a negative fecal exam prior to breeding. Furthermore, be sure that you are feeding your female the very best nutritionally. (NOTE: If you are feeding your female the diet as described above, then you can be sure that she is getting the proper nutrition.) Some breeders will add puppy kibble to the mother's diet to ensure that the developing fetuses are getting the building blocks of nutrients they need to grow into healthy pups. Most experts agree that the proper diet is one that provides large amounts of protein and fat with a mixture of whole grains.

Dachshund dams usually carry their pups between sixty and sixty-five days. (If the mother has passed the sixty-five-day mark, then you need to get the mother to the vet as there is likely a problem.) You will also want to have taken the mother to the veterinarian for an x-ray or ultrasound which can tell you how many pups to expect. This will help during whelping; if one pup cannot be passed through the birth canal, your vet will need to intervene surgically. (NOTE: If your vet needs to perform a cesarean section to deliver the pups, he or she is likely to go ahead with spaying your female. This is standard procedure.)

In addition, you will need to ensure that you supplement your female's diet particularly between weeks two and four of the puppies' lives. It is at this time that the mother must produce the most milk for the rapidly developing pups.

Some breeders take their Dachshund pups in for a vet visit at two weeks and again at four weeks. In addition, the breeder generally gives the first round of vaccinations to the pups at six weeks. You will need to prepare for the financial aspects of this.

Some breeders will weigh the pups using a postal scale to ensure that the puppies are steadily gaining weight. A pup that does not put on weight properly should get special attention. (Pups should gain some weight daily, even if only a few ounces.)

While there are many rewards involved in breeding and raising Doxies, there are also many risks to both the mother and the pups. However, being available during the whelping time and having the ability to be with the pups and monitor their growth will provide a great reward to you.

Figure 21 Adorable Dachshund pups

CHAPTER 9

What is Involved in Showing Dachshunds?

So, you have purchased your perfect pup, and you are convinced that he is a show quality dog. Anyone can show a dog provided that the dog is purebred and registered with the proper club. (The American Kennel Club is generally the most dominant organization for registering dogs; however, there is also another club in the United States known as the Continental Kennel Club. However, only dogs registered with the AKC may participate in that organization's shows.)

In order to prepare for showing your Doxie, it is first recommended to attend some dog shows so that you can get a feel for what show dogs are required to do. Next, start networking. Talk with those participating in the show. They are usually happy to help you get prepared for showing your pup. In addition, you may be able to find a show ring mentor who will gladly advise you on the steps to take in getting ready to show your Dachshund.

NOTE: Your Dachshund must be registered with the American Kennel Club AND be at least six months old in order to be eligible for dog shows. Dogs entered in the shows may not be spayed or neutered, and they must conform to AKC standards.

At every AKC-sponsored dog show, a club table will be set up. It is here that you can gather even more information about showing your Dachshund. Furthermore, the American Kennel Club and the Dachshund Club of America also offer classes for beginner dog conformation contenders. In these classes, you will learn all about breed standards and the expectation of the judges during a dog show.

You should also be encouraged to sign up for and participate in novice dog shows held at local clubs in your area. These dog shows (known as match shows) give beginning dog handlers the experience necessary to prepare them for more important shows later on.

Certainly, you may decide that your dog has the right stuff for the show ring, but you are not interested in handling the pup during confirmation shows. Perhaps you do not feel qualified enough. Have no fear! You can always hire a professional handler who has a wealth of experience to show your star puppy! Go about choosing a professional handler is much the same way you would learn how to show the dog yourself. Attend shows. Talk to other dog owners. Get recommendations. Always feel free to ask questions of the potential handler. He or she will be working closely with your pride and joy, and you want their relationship to be as productive as if you are the one in the show ring with him.

Figure 22 Dachshunds participating in a dog show

CHAPTER 10
Senior Dachshunds

Remember, a Dachshund can live to sixteen years of age on average, perhaps more! Caring for a senior Doxie is just as important as caring for a young Dachshund pup. Certainly, it may take some adjusting, but it is oh, so worth it for your precious companion.

First, you will need to make adjustments to your Doxie's diet. You may notice that your Dachshund does not enjoy the same food he has enjoyed – and wolfed down – for years. So, changes are in order! As your Doxie ages, he will experience a lower energy level. You will need to change his diet to compensate for this. He will no longer need as much fat and protein as he once did. An older Doxie will need more glucosamine (which could be given as a supplement). He will also need more calcium and fiber in his diet. (As the Dachshund ages, his digestive system slows down. Sufficient fiber ensures that his system works as it should. This may also be given as a supplement.)

Second, you will need to take into consideration the type of flooring you have in your home. Those once strong, powerful legs may often become arthritic. Your beloved Doxie may have a harder time getting up from a prone position. What does this have to do with your flooring? It is more difficult for an aging dog to get up from a tile or otherwise slick floor surface than it is to get up from a carpeted area.

(NOTE: Be cautious when giving your Doxie a bath in the tub. The slick bottom of the tub can be hazardous to an older Dachshund. He may slip on the wet porcelain and become injured.)

Third, the Dachshund is often prone to arthritis and the stiff joints characteristic of the ailment. If you live in a colder area, your Doxie may be even more susceptible to the effects of stiff joints. In order to combat this painful condition, you can give your Dachshund the aforementioned glucosamine, chondroitin, MSM, or fish oil in an effort to promote healthy joints. Some senior dog foods are formulated with these minerals already included in the food. You may need to give these minerals to your dog in the form of supplements. If this is the method you choose, you are in luck! There are many tasty treats that incorporate the above minerals. They are chewable, and the dog readily takes the supplements.

Next, you should ensure that your dog has regular vet visits. At each visit, you will need to ask that lab work including blood tests and other regular preventative tests are performed. It is always best to catch any issues early before a health problem progresses into something that can't be treated.

Don't be surprised if your Doxie becomes lumpier as he ages. Generally, all dogs develop fatty tumors and/or cysts anywhere and everywhere on his body. These are generally not harmful at all. Of course, it is not a bad idea to have your vet check any lumps out just to be careful.

Expect your Doxie's eyesight to worsen as he ages. Cataracts are not uncommon in a variety of breeds, and the Dachshund is no different. To be honest, there are really no necessary adjustments should your dog lose his sight. If you have had your Doxie for the majority of his life, he will be able to rely on his other senses in order to get around. You may also notice that he can't hear as well as he once did. Again, there is very little you can do to make this any better for the dog. Certainly, you have never allowed your Doxie to go outdoors without a leash. Continue this habit so that he will not dash into traffic that he can no longer hear.

Experts caution owners of senior Doxies to be careful about startling your dog when he is resting. He may or may not feel the vibration of your feet and be prepared for your presence. If frightened, he may nip you – it is not characteristic of him, but it is basically a response to being scared. You may have to shout his name in order to wake him, but at least this will not scare him as much as waking him from a nap with no warning.

Finally, remember that your Doxie still wants to play with you, and he may be getting older, but he is still capable of learning new tricks! He may tire a little more easily, but your Dachshund still craves playtime with you. You may need to shorten play time into fifteen-minute intervals but continue to play with your Dachshund each day. This will make him happy, and it will keep his muscles toned. In addition, it can actually promote joint health by keeping them supple.

The most important thing is to keep your dog as happy and healthy as possible in his golden years. Provide him with the proper diet, get him to the vet for regular check-ups, and keep him reasonably active. Your senior Doxie will thank you for it!

Figure 23 A senior Doxie, notice the graying muzzle

CHAPTER 11

What Will Training a Dachshund Include?

I asked a friend who owned a pair of Dachshunds what it was like to train them. She replied, "It isn't much different from raising children!" While the Doxie is reputed to be rather stubborn, a patient person committed to working with a Doxie will achieve training success. Dachshunds respond better to training with positive reinforcements rather than negative punishments. One Dachshund pet parent lamented that housebreaking the Doxie is a lifelong process. However, patience and persistence will pay off when working with the badger dog.

Dachshund Puppy Training

When working with any breed of puppy, consistency is key. Also, the older your pup is when you bring him home (and begin training), the better your efforts will be rewarded. Next, particularly with Doxies, you will want to develop a reward system. Often, this involves praise and treats. While you might be tempted to punish your pup for having an accident in the house, you must refrain from such! Instead, praise him and give him a treat when he does potty in the proper place. By using positive reinforcement, he will learn much more quickly than you realize!

First, you should not attempt to take your puppy outdoors for potty training. One, he has not had all his vaccinations prevented parvovirus at this point. Parvovirus lives on the ground, and even extreme temperatures – not even freezing temperatures – will kill the virus. So, it is important not to take your puppy outside until he has at least had the twelve-week-old set of immunizations.

I'm sure you are wondering how to begin potty training if you shouldn't take your pup outdoors at this point. This is when you need to utilize puppy pads. Puppy pads are sheets of cotton with a plastic backing that absorbs urine. Most puppy pads are also formulated with pheromones which attract the puppy to use the bathroom on the pad rather than some random place on the floor.

I would be remiss if I did not add here that a dog is really not prepared to be away from its mother and being housebroken until it is at least eight weeks old. You will notice between eight and twelve weeks that the puppy gains more and more control of his bladder each week. If you wait until a puppy is at least eight weeks old before bringing him home with you, you will have an easier time housebreaking him.

Expect to be up and down with your puppy the first two weeks after you bring him home. Again, as he ages, his bathroom schedule will become more predictable. There is a way to work on night-time potty breaks that involve crate training.

I prefer a wire crate that comes with a removable tray at the bottom of the structure. This tray is imperative to training. You can put a puppy pad in the tray, and, should there be an overflow of waste in the tray, you can always remove it for easy cleaning. Next, place your pup's bedding in one corner of the crate. A dog will not usually use the bathroom where it eats or sleeps (of course, there is always an exception to this, but it is rare). Place water in another corner. Should your pup need to use the bathroom at night while you are asleep, he has the puppy pad to use. A puppy, especially a Dachshund, is so small that his crate will give him plenty of room to be away from the used area of the puppy pad. Keep a fresh puppy pad in his crate at all times. You may notice that he walks into his crate to use the bathroom after a few weeks of this routine.

Once your Doxie pup has had his twelve-week vaccinations, then you can feel more at ease with taking him outside to potty. I recommend taking him out after meals and each time he wakes from a nap. I have done this with my own dogs, and as soon as they finish eating, they automatically go to the front door, ready for a walk. Yes, there will be accidents, but, give the pup praise for what he does correctly. Once you begin taking him outside to potty, when he is successful, give him a treat when he comes back inside. A word to the wise, you may find yourself waiting quite a while during the first few weeks of potty training. But, if you will have a treat ready when he does use the bathroom, he will soon learn what you expect of him.

You might be surprised just how quickly your Doxie picks up housebreaking if you use a treat-reward method. He will notice that he does NOT get a treat for using the bathroom in an unwelcome place (i.e., off the puppy pad). By reinforcing good behavior, the pup will learn what you expect of him, and he will try to live up to that expectation. Remember to take your pup outside at roughly the same time every day. Give him verbal praise for a job well done in addition to a tasty treat. These are the things that he remembers, and they make housebreaking so much easier!

Dachshund Dog Harness and Leash Training

I also recommend beginning leash training at the same time as you start housebreaking. Some pet parents put a harness on their dogs at a very young age, and they do not take the harness off. If your pup is comfortable with wearing the harness, and there are no skin irritations – then there is nothing wrong with keeping the harness on your Doxie as well. This will help in leash training as you do not have to stop to put the harness on him each time you are ready to go outside.

When you take him out – provided he has had his preventative vaccinations – then set him down on the ground. Take a step and coax him to follow you. Give him a treat for doing so, and repeat. Leash training, when started at the appropriate time, is very easy. You may want to get him used to the idea of walking on the leash and realizing that he must stop before you begin teaching him to heel and stay. Remember, the Dachshund will need to be leashed any time he goes outdoors. Work with him so that he accepts this while he is young. The Doxie is such a smart pup; he may eventually learn to bring the leash to you when he desires some outdoor fun!

Dachshund Crate/Kennel Training

I am a firm believer in crate training. You see, many pups experience separation anxiety. If you leave for work or even for an errand, a pup experiencing this awful condition may become destructive. For many pups, the enclosed space of a crate or kennel provides a sense of security and helps to curb separation anxiety.

I personally prefer a wire crate over a large plastic crate. In my opinion, the wire crate provides the security of an enclosure while being open enough that the pup can see his surroundings. Again, the wire crate often has a removable tray at the bottom which makes any possible clean-ups quite easy. If you worry that your pup might become cold in the wire crate, there are cloth covers that you can purchase and place over the crate. However, if your home is a comfortable temperature while you are away, and your pup has his favorite blanket, he will be quite warm inside the wire crate.

Previously, I mentioned crate training as a means of potty training your pup. However, before you begin housebreaking your dog, you want to get him comfortable with the crate (NOTE: for me, the terms crate and kennel are interchangeable). In order to get the dog used to the crate – and to ensure that he actually views the crate as a comforting place – then a little work is in order. Begin by placing a trail of treats leading into the crate. As he goes in on his own, praise him. I would not shut the door on him just yet. Once you have mastered the idea that going into the crate is rewarding, then you can begin closing the door and leaving the area for two to four minutes at a time. Work your way up to five minutes in the crate with no whining. Any time you come to take your pup out of the crate, make a big deal of your return. (All pet parents speak to their dog upon returning home, right? You greet him as if he is a family member you haven't seen all day, correct?) Soon, your pup will associate the crate with a positive place, and he will be happy to see you come home and remove him from the crate as well.

Be sure to place a favorite toy inside the crate. This will also help with the adjustment of spending time in the crate.

NOTE: Previously in this chapter, I mentioned keeping the harness on your dog at all times for ease of housebreaking. I absolutely recommend that you remove the harness any time your pup is going to be locked in the crate. While a properly fitted harness is not likely to snag on any part of the crate, there is always a first time for everything. So, to err on the side of caution, remove the harness before crating your pup, especially if you are heading out to run errands or go to work. An ounce of prevention is worth so much more than a pound of cure.

CHAPTER 12

What are Some Examples of Dachshund Mixes?

Certainly, when combining two awesome purebred dogs, you expect to get the best of both breeds! Often, when creating a hybrid breed using the Dachshund, the resulting pups will still have a somewhat elongated body. They also tend to inherit the long muzzle of the Dachshund. Of course, no one can predict exactly what a Doxie mix will look like; however, one can be sure that any resulting pups will inherit the tenacious spirit of their Dachshund parent!

Dachshund Beagle Mix

The Dachshund and Beagle Mix is actually a rather popular hybrid breed. (Hybrid breed means putting two purebred dogs together to mate.) Known as the Doxle, this hybrid breed is becoming increasingly well-known. The American Kennel Club is actually recognizing the presence of the Doxle (however this does not mean that the AKC is registering the hybrid breed,). You might also hear this hybrid referred to as a "Beaschund" or a "Beagle/Weiner." The Doxle has the elongated body of the Dachshund parent, and it also sports the characteristic short legs of the Dachshund. The Doxle will usually have the face of the Beagle parent, and he will usually measure about nine to twelve inches in height. Weight is between twenty to thirty pounds at maturity. The Doxle may be white with a tricolor pattern, solid brown, black and tan, or solid black. The average life expectancy of the Doxle is twelve to fourteen years. He should have relatively no health problems other than those associated with an elongated spine. Joint issues are often a point of contention for the Doxle as well. Doxles are just as happy indoors as they are outdoors; however, because he will not be a large dog, it is best that he lives inside with his family. He will be a highly intelligent dog, and he will enjoy learning new tricks every day. He is eager to please his handler, and this makes him more apt to learning commands. Remember, both the Dachshund and the Beagle are hunting hounds. The prey drive will be extremely strong with the Doxle. He will also need to be leashed any time he is outdoors. The Doxle will enjoy spending time with the family, and he may expect to be at the center of family activities. The Doxle is most definitely a great combination of two wonderful breeds.

Dachshund Terrier Mix

The Dachshund Terrier Mix is a combination of the Doxie with any kind of terrier – the Rat Terrier, the Yorkshire Terrier, the Silky Terrier or even a Boston Terrier. In this instance, you will see the resulting hybrid puppies exhibit characteristics much like a typical terrier. This means that the Dachshund Terrier mix will often be stubborn, tenacious, and ferociously loyal. Depending on what specific type of terrier is bred with a Dachshund, a Dachshund-Terrier mix will have a variation of names. A Dachshund bred with a Yorkshire Terrier is generally known as a

Dorkie, and a Dachshund mixed with a Scottish Terrier is known as a Doxie Scott. A Dachshund Terrier often sports a dapple patterned coat. The Dachshund-Terrier mix will often sport an elongated body much like that of the Doxie parent. Expect a Dachshund-Terrier mix to enjoy digging; unfortunately, it is a trait present in both the Doxie and most all terrier breeds! The Dachshund-Terrier mix is often very friendly and rarely meets a stranger! They are generally playful and energetic as well. They tend to bond with the person who trains them as they spend the most time together. They are also excellent guardians, and they do not hesitate to bark at anything they feel is amiss. All in all, the Dachshund Terrier loves to cuddle. They make great lap dogs! They also tend to suffer from separation anxiety while their owners are away, so they are a better fit for someone who is home regularly.

Corgi Dachshund Mix

The Corgi and Dachshund mix is another rather popular hybrid breed. Known as the Dorgi, this loveable mixed breed is longer than he is tall (much like his Doxie parent!). The Dorgi looks much like a Corgi with an elongated body and long muzzle. He will often have wiry, medium-length hair that is one of several possible colors: black, light brown or golden, black and tan, dark brown or chocolate, and brown and white. Often, there will be a white spot on the chest of the Dorgi. Many times, he sports the long, erect ears of the Corgi. He generally weighs between fifteen and twenty-eight pounds, and he is roughly the same height as the Dachshund parent breed. He is very loving, highly intelligent, and full of energy. He is outgoing and never meets a stranger. He is great with children, and he will bark if he feels that someone or something is threatening his family and/or their territory.

French Bulldog Dachshund

Known as a French Bulldog Weiner mix, this interesting pairing of breeds makes for a unique hybrid dog! The French Bulldog Weiner mix is often fourteen inches in height at the shoulder (this is a little bit larger than some of the other Dachshund mixes). He often weighs about fifty pounds. Exact numbers will be dependent, of course, upon the immediate puppy parents. The French Bulldog Weiner mix is often very friendly, and he loves his humans more than anything. He loves all the individuals in his family (the Doxie pet parent tends to bond to one person in a family even if he is loving with them all). He could be quite feisty, and he is likely to be an independent thinker. He may be able to get into things that you never expected – such as ripping into dog food bags. Overall, the French Bulldog Weiner mix is a highly affectionate dog who wants nothing more than to spend time with his human family.

English Dachshund

This hybrid breed is known as the Miniature English Bulldach. This adorable designer breed truly has the best of both its parent breeds. The Bulldach will be very small. He is likely to have short, powerful legs. He is known for being both brave and loyal to his family. He will need regular exercise to stay healthy – both Doxies and English Bulldogs have a tendency to gain weight. Common colors of the English Bulldach include black, brown, white, black and tan, or silver.

Other Dachshund Mixes

The Dachshound – yes, you read that correctly – is a mixture of the Dachshund and the Basset Hound. These two breeds are already quite alike, so mixing the two breeds is quite plausible. Both have a long and low-to-the-ground body (so, of course, you expect the Dachshound to have a body much like the Doxie parent breed). In fact, the Dachshound looks like a slightly longer version of the Doxie.

The Doxiepin is a combination of the Dachshund and the Miniature Pinscher. This absolutely adorable hybrid breed often looks like a Mini Pin with a longer body. The Doxiepin will often be black and tan, or rusty red. The ears will be erect, and he will often be a little more stocky than either of the parent breeds.

The Papshund is a hybrid combining the Dachshund and the Papillon. The Papshund often has the long hair of the Papillon parent breed. The Papshund will be taller than his Doxie parent, and often he will be overwhelmingly white in color. The Papshund is often purported to be friendlier and less timid, than the Dachshund pet parent.

The Goldenshund is a gorgeous little hybrid! A mixture of the Golden Retriever and the Dachshund, the Goldenshund often looks like a very small Golden Retriever with the short, stocky legs of the Doxie and the golden locks of the Goldie parent breed. This particular hybrid breed will need a great deal of exercise, and is recommended most for families that are active outdoors.

The Doxbull is a hybrid breed combining the Dachshund and the Pit Bull. While exact coat colors are dependent on the immediate parents, the Doxbull often sports a beautiful brindle coat. He will be somewhat aloof around other dogs, and most experts suggest early socialization in order to promote friendly behavior in your Doxbull.

The Dameranian is a combination of the Dachshund and the Pomeranian. Crossing the Doxie with a Pomeranian often brings about a pup that is much easier to train than his Dachshund parent breed. He will often have gorgeous, long, red-gold hair. His chest may be white, as is his stomach. His ears are likely to be long and sport feathery hair. His muzzle is more like the Doxie parent.

The Chiweenie is another popular Dachshund hybrid breed. The Chiweenie is a combination of the Dachshund and a Chihuahua. The Chiweenie will often be rather small, like the Chihuahua parent. Unlike other Doxie hybrids, the Chiweenie may have either long or short hair. He may also have one of two head shapes. Predicting what a Chiweenie will look like is difficult, due to these factors.

The Doxiepoo is a hybrid breed combining a miniature Poodle and a Dachshund. The Poodle parent influence helps make a Doxiepoo hypoallergenic, and the personality of the Poodle parent makes the Doxiepoo quite easy to train. This is especially wonderful when you consider the chief complaint of Dachshund owners is the stubbornness they encounter in the Doxie. The Doxiepoo will be small, and he is generally a delightful little dog.

The Daimaraner is a gorgeous cross between a Dachshund and a Weimaraner. Often possessing the soulful light-colored eyes of the Weimaraner parent, the Daimaraner is often a light color (generally gray). He is rather short, and he possesses the elongated body of the Dachshund. Both breeds are hunters at heart, so expect a high prey drive from the Daimaraner. The Daimaraner is an independent little pup who enjoys cuddling but is just as happy spending time on his own.

The Labshund is a hybrid breed resulting from breeding a Labrador Retriever and a Dachshund. The Labshund will be a shorter version of the Labrador Retriever. He will often have the long, thick tail of the Labrador Retriever, and he is smart and loving. He requires a good bit of exercise, so the Labshund needs an active family.

One final interesting hybrid breed is the Dachmation. This is a combination of the Dalmatian and the Dachshund. This small pup will inherit the short, stubby legs of the Dachshund and the sweet spots of the Dalmatian parent. He will be very friendly with his family but might be aloof around strangers.

Figure 24 The playful antics of the Dachshund will keep you entertained

Conclusion

You will have many wonderful years ahead with your precious Doxie! Within this book, I have discussed any and all aspects regarding choosing, living with, and maximizing your experience with the breed. Yes, the Dachshund can be stubborn, but it is his tenacity that makes him such a great hunter. It is also his persistence that makes him so entertaining. Once you bond with your Dachshund, you have a friend for the rest of his life! He will entertain you and your friends with his silly antics. He will also curl up in your lap for cuddles just when you need it the most. He is a great watchdog, and although he is small – and unlikely to deter an intruder through size alone – he will most definitely let you know that someone has entered his territory!

Properly cared for, your Doxie will experience fairly good health. He is also apt to live for the better part of two decades, with the tender loving care that only you can provide. Whether you decide to purchase a Dachshund pup, or you decide to adopt an older Doxie, your life will only become better for owning a Doxie! Congratulations on your new fur baby. May the both of you have wonderful memories for years to come!

Your Trusted Dachshund Resource List

Dachshund Breeders in the USA

- http://www.bbdox.com/

  Located in Maryville, TN, the Busy B's Doxie Breeding establishment is set in a small community on the outskirts of Chattanooga. This family breeding business offers all types of Dachshund pups – short and long-haired varieties, wirehaired Doxies, and specialty color pattern Doxies as well. They specialize in miniature Dachshunds also.

- http://www.downhomedachshunds.com/

  Located in South Mississippi, Downhome Dachshunds offers Doxie pups of all sizes and coat colors. Their AKC approved kennels are a part of a family breeding business. Each Doxie puppy is given a great deal of love and socialization before it is ever offered for sale.

- http://www.maydersdachshunds.com/

  Mayders Dachshunds is also a family run business located in Pennsylvania. This breeder specializes in long-haired Doxies. They do have a waiting list, so interested individuals are encouraged to fill out an application and get approved for the waiting list.

- http://www.momsdachshunds.com/

  Located in Ohio, Mom's Dachshunds is another family owned breeding business offering all sizes and color pattern Dachshunds. Most definitely a breeder who seeks to improve the Doxie, Mom's Dachshunds are bred for health and temperament. Mom does not allow her pups to leave the facility before they are nine weeks old, and pups will be wormed and receive their first round of vaccinations before going to their forever home.

- http://www.judykaydachshunds.com/

  Judy Kay's Dachshunds breeding facility is located in Weatherford, Texas. This facility offers AKC Dachshunds. However, if you are considering showing or breeding your Doxie in the future, you might want to consider another breeder as this facility specializes in strictly companion animals. This facility expects to screen potential buyers, and the breeder welcomes anyone wishing to give a Doxie a good home to visit her facility.

- http://cookswieners.com/

  The Low Rider Doxies Breeding Kennel is located in Dunbar, Pennsylvania. This AKC approved kennel boasts thirty years of breeding experience. This family-owned kennel is run by a husband and wife team, and they strive to give pups a great deal of love and socialization before they go to their forever homes. This breeder ships all over the United States via Continental Airlines.

- http://www.arizonagroundhounds.com/

  Arizona Ground Hounds is a breeding facility which also sells companion animals only (no breeding rights). Those purchasing from this facility will be given a health contract, and the breeder offers to ship across the United States. Puppies are socialized from a young age, and they are also vaccinated and receive an initial worming treatment before they leave the facility.

- http://dandydoxdachshunds.com/

  Located in Redding, California, the DandyDox Dachshunds breeding facility is an American Kennel Club Breeder of Merit award winners. The breeders specialize in miniature Dachshunds, and they also participate in mini Dachshund exhibition shows.

- http://hounds.homestead.com/

  High Sierra Dachshunds is located in northern California and is convenient to areas such as Reno, Nevada. This breeding facility is known for breeding, and training AKC registered Doxies. The breeder is quite particular about the forever homes of its pups (note: the breeder only sells to select homes). The breeder offers a health guarantee, and according to her website, a lifetime of support for those who take home one of her pups.

- http://dachshunddapplecreamca.com/

  Cloud 9 Breeding Facility is located in Southern California. A small breeding facility, Cloud 9 offers only two or three litters a year. These show-quality dogs may be either a smooth-coat or of the long-haired variety.

Dachshund Breeders in Canada

- http://freestyle14.ca/

  Freestyle Retrievers is a breeding facility which specializes in Labrador Retrievers and wire-haired Miniature Dachshunds. Freestyle Retrievers has been raising and showing this special type of Doxie for twenty years. This facility is located in Ontario.

- http://heavenlyhund.com/

  Heavenly Hund breeding facility is also located in Ontario, Canada. According to the owner, hounds are their lives, and not their business. The breeder touts thirty-five years of experience, both in breeding and working with Doxies in the show ring. One will find long-haired and smooth-haired Dachshunds at this facility; however, they do strive to develop varieties of the cream-colored Doxie.

- http://www.classicdachshunds.com/

  Classic Dachshunds is located approximately two hours from Toronto, Ontario. They are a licensed kennel, and the breeders strive to maintain the beauty of the classic miniature long-haired Dachshund.

- https://www.sniffntellkennels.com

  Located in Ontario, Sniff N Tell Kennels breeds show quality Doxies. They specialize in long-haired Dachshunds and Smooth-haired Doxies. While they only offer puppies occasionally, the pup will come with a health guarantee and contract.

- http://www.pawprintsminidachshunds.com/

  This Canadian breeder of both long- and smooth-coated
  Doxies is also located in Ontario. These show quality pups
  come from a long line of happy, healthy, and championship
  Doxie parents. The breeder has forty years of experience, and,
  while a small facility, those purchasing from this breeder will
  be assured a quality pup.

- https://nanaimodachshunds.com/

  Nanaimo Dachshunds is a small, home-based breeder who
  strives for quality Doxies "with funky colors." The breeder has
  thirty years of experience and desires for her pups to go only
  to new homes. She is located in British Columbia, Canada on
  Vancouver Island.

- http://www.livingskiesdachshunds.com/

  This breeder of Dachshunds is located in Saskatchewan,
  Canada. The in-home breeding facility is dedicated to raising
  healthy pups with a sweet temperament.

- https://www.rosehilldachshunds.com/

  This Alberta, Canada breeder specializes in long-haired
  Miniature Dachshunds. They state that they occasionally have
  puppies, and they are willing to ship puppies to prospective
  buyers.

- http://www.pamadron.ca/

  This Ontario-based breeder is located in the Thousand
  Islands region of the area. The facility specializes in breeding
  Miniature Long-haired Dachshunds for not only health and
  temperament but for "brains and beauty" as well.

- http://teckeldunord.com/

  This breeder is located in Quebec, Canada. The breeder has consulted various geneticists and other experts to avoid breeding for specific colors that might carry health risks. The breeder specializes in long-haired Miniature Dachshunds.

Dachshund Breeders and UK Resources

- https://www.thekennelclub.org.uk/services

  The Kennel Club of United Kingdom offers a wealth of assured breeder names as well as location and contact information. The link above can be followed to find lists of breeders, and the list is broken into varying categories such as long-haired, smooth-haired, and wire-haired.

- https://dachshundbreedcouncil.wordpress.com

  This website also provides a list of reputable breeders associated with the breed council in the United Kingdom.

- https://www.dardaxdachshunds.com

  This small breeding facility offers miniature long-haired Doxies.

- http://dachshund.rescueshelter.com/uk

  This website offers a list of shelters with Dachshunds available for adoption in the United Kingdom.

Made in the USA
Coppell, TX
18 May 2020

26014659R00066